the **PASSPORT** PROGRAM

the **PASSPORT** PROGRAM

A Journey through
Emotional, Social,
Cognitive, and
Self-Development

GRADES
1-5

ANN VERNON

Research Press • 2612 North Mattis Avenue • Champaign, Illinois 61822

CONTENTS

Grade 1

SELF-DEVELOPMENT

EMOTIONAL DEVELOPMENT

SOCIAL DEVELOPMENT

COGNITIVE DEVELOPMENT

Grade 2

Grade 3

Grade 4

Grade 5

HANDOUTS

Grade 1

Grade 2

Grade 3

Grade 4

Grade 5

FOREWORD

In the early 1970s, Rational-Emotive Education was a gleam in the eye of Albert Ellis. One of its earliest implementations was in the Living School, a pioneering school run by the Institute for Rational Living in New York City.

Since that time, giant leaps have been made by educators and mental health professionals in using rational thinking and emotional self-management skills to foster positive mental health in children and adolescents. Among the very richest and most creative contributions have been made by Ann Vernon, one of this country's outstanding counselor educators, whose two previous volumes of Rational-Emotive Education curricula are in wide use in schools and counseling offices throughout the U.S. and abroad.

In this important new work, Dr. Vernon brings her understanding of how to help youngsters become happy, self-accepting, and well-functioning adults into the future. Today's children face not only normal developmental problems, but also a myriad of potentially overwhelming stressors unimaginable in previous generations. As educators, parents, and mental health professionals, we will surely need all the resources we can muster to help safeguard our children from self-downing, irrational thinking, debilitating emotions, and self-defeating behaviors.

A unique aspect of this book is that it offers an array of vignettes of real-life issues applicable to youngsters of all cultural and socioeconomic backgrounds. Situations dealt with range from doing poorly on a test and handling unfairness and rejection through coping with disruptive family situations and being tempted by drug-experimenting peers. Dr. Vernon is superb at entering children's and adolescents' experiential worlds. Many of the vignettes in the series are eloquent first-person accounts by the youngsters themselves, talking about their struggles and how they were able to use rational thinking skills to help them increase self-acceptance, deal with troublesome emotions, and overcome self-defeating behaviors. Engaging "lessons"–adaptable for both classroom or counseling settings–each present a developmentally appropriate stimulus activity, skills for dealing with this stimulus, and follow-up questions and activities that allow youngsters to make the transition from intellectual insight to direct application of concepts and skills in their own lives.

This highly practical resource will be a great boon to all who wish to help grow a crop of children and adolescents who are secure in themselves and their values, resilient and flexible in dealing with life's stressors and challenges, and able to relate effectively and responsibly to others and pursue their dreams.

JANET L. WOLFE, PH.D.
EXECUTIVE DIRECTOR
ALBERT ELLIS INSTITUTE

ACKNOWLEDGMENTS

This book and its companion volumes for grades 6–8 and grades 9–12 are the result of a conviction that we cannot leave the challenges of growing up to chance. Rather, we need to systematically teach children and adolescents how to navigate each stage of development so that they don't give up before they grow up. In my estimation there is no better way to do that than to teach young people how to apply the principles of Rational-Emotive Behavior Therapy to the problems of growing up. I have been using REBT with children and adolescents for many years and want to acknowledge Albert Ellis, Janet Wolfe, Ray DiGiuseppe, and Dominic DiMattia for sharing their knowledge and expertise with me and for supporting my efforts to apply these concepts in educational settings.

I want to thank my colleague David Martino for his thorough review and critique of my material, as well as for his contribution of two stories for this book. In addition, appreciation goes to Maria Colombo for contributing several activities for the social and cognitive development sections and to the school counselors, many of whom are my former students, who piloted these materials and offered helpful suggestions.

A big thank-you goes to the Research Press staff–Ann Wendel, Russ Pence, and Karen Steiner–for enthusiastically endorsing this project and supporting me throughout the process with their helpful suggestions. It is indeed a pleasure to work with them.

Last but not least, I want to express appreciation to the parents of my clients, who trusted me with the privilege of working with their children and adolescents in my private counseling practice. My utmost gratitude goes to the young people who have been my clients. Many of the ideas in these volumes originated from work I did with them. The lessons they taught me have been invaluable, and it has been gratifying to see how they can think, feel, and behave in healthier ways as a result of intervention. The stories in the present volume are all based on actual experiences children shared with me. The stories and poems in the two companion volumes are all written by adolescents, who hoped that "telling their stories" would help other kids their age through the developmental process.

INTRODUCTION: THE DEVELOPMENTAL PERSPECTIVE

That was then; this is now. Some things change, and some things stay the same. These two phrases accurately describe some of what I think about when I reflect on child and adolescent development. In some ways, being a young person today is significantly different than it was when many of us were growing up. Back then, we used drugs if we had a physical illness. Now many young people use drugs to numb their emotional pain. Back then, violence was something that occasionally happened in big cities. Now violence is everywhere and has a tremendous impact on the lives of children and adolescents. Back then, child and adolescent depression was rare. Now it is almost an epidemic. Back then, most families were like the Cleavers in *Leave It to Beaver.* Now most children grow up in dual-worker families, and many of them at some point in their lives live in single-parent or blended family structures. Back then, you rarely heard about child or adolescent suicide. Now it is the second leading cause of death among adolescents.

These comparisons could go on and on. In some ways, life for children and adolescents is very different. And in other ways, many of the issues are the same. I recall a discussion with my son the summer after his senior year in high school. He was complaining about having to go to Wisconsin for a family vacation. "Mom, you just don't understand. I want to stay home with my friends because it's my last summer and my friends are really important to me. I don't want to miss out on everything by being gone." He seemed convinced that I wouldn't understand, but his statements brought back a flood of memories. Without saying a word, I went to my file and pulled out a letter I had written to my mother the summer after my senior year in high school, when we were having a discussion about going to our cabin. I handed it to Eric. "Dear Mom," the letter read. "I just have to stay home this summer. You know there is nothing for me to do at the cabin. You probably can't imagine it, but kids my age want action. We can't help it; that's just the way we are. I've got to be with my friends. Please don't make me go."

After that, nothing more was said. Eric, his father, and I negotiated the amount of time Eric would be gone, and I don't imagine he really missed out on any more than I did by being "away from the action" for a few days. But of course neither one of us saw it that way when we were 18 years old. This is just one example of how some things stay the same, and as I listen to children and adolescents express their thoughts and feelings to me in counseling sessions, I am repeatedly reminded of the fact that developmental stages have remained relatively constant.

It is imperative that we know about developmental stages and characteristics. Without an understanding of what growing up is all about, we run the risk of overreacting or underreacting to problematic symptoms; we may not see a situation for what it truly is. This point hit home for me when I was listening to an audiotape presented by one of my practicum students. My student believed her client might be in an abusive relationship with her mother. "Let's listen to the tape," I said to my student. And as I listened, I heard a 15-year-old young woman describing her conflictual relationship with her mother. She spoke about how her mother never let her do anything, was always yelling at her, and was continually forcing her to do things she didn't want to do. I asked my student if she had probed for specific examples, explaining that it is very characteristic for young adolescents to overgeneralize and approach everything dichotomously: Either they get to do everything, or they get to do nothing, for example. I certainly did not want to imply that an abusive relationship was out of the question in this case, but I cautioned my student to look at the problem through multiple lenses and to ask for specific examples and take into account what we know about adolescent females–that many have love-hate relationships with their mothers, that they usually feel oppressed, and that they generally don't want to be forced to do anything they don't want to because this thwarts their growing need for independence. My student went back to her counselee, armed with new perspectives. Over the course of several sessions, including an interview with the client and her mother, it became apparent that this case exemplified typical adolescent issues, not an abusive relationship.

Developmental characteristics not only need to be taken into account when assessing problems, they also need to be considered as we look at how young people interpret events. One third grader wrote a will to designate which friends would get his prized possessions in case something happened to him. His parents were understandably concerned, thinking their son might be contemplating suicide. As it turned out, he wrote a will because his teacher had been sharing a current event about children who had been trapped in a cave. This youngster assumed that if something like that could happen to other children, it might happen to him, and he wanted to make sure his friends received his favorite things. Younger children interpret things very literally because they are concrete thinkers. In this case, cognitive development limited the way this child interpreted his situation, and these limitations in turn influenced his behavior.

We must also remember that despite the fact that the developmental stages and characteristics haven't changed much over the decades, what has changed are the cultural and social factors that affect the lives of young people. Children in today's society grow up faster. As Mary Pipher, author of *Reviving Ophelia,* notes, "The protected place in space and time that we once called childhood has grown shorter" (1994, p. 28). Now, in addition to dealing with typical growing-up issues, which in themselves can be challenging and confusing, children and adolescents have much more to cope with. Many grow up in poverty, are victims of abuse, or struggle with parental divorce or remarriage. Superimpose these problems on top of the normal growing-up problems, and it is no wonder that far too many young people deal with their issues in unhealthy ways. In part, unhealthy responses also reflect developmental capabilities. For young adolescents, whose sense of time is the here and now and whose thinking is still for the most part concrete, numbing pain with drugs and alcohol seems like the easiest thing to do when life becomes overwhelming. They may not have the ability to carefully consider consequences.

The frightening thing about how children and adolescents cope with developmental as well as situational problems is that the long-term consequences may have a profoundly negative impact on their lives. But because they live in the present and aren't able to project far into the future, many young people deal with these stressors the best they can, given their level of development. In other words, if they don't have the ability to take other perspectives or see alternatives, it is often difficult for them to use the good judgment we as adults think they should be capable of employing. We need to remember that young people interpret their world differently than we do.

Although many young people are able to meet the challenges of growing up, we can probably remember from our own experience wondering if we were "normal"–if what was happening to us was typical. I see my clients breathe a sigh of relief when I reassure them that they are normal and help them understand why they are thinking, feeling, and behaving the way they are, given their level of development. It seems to me that we take too much for granted, assuming that young people somehow know what is normal, when in fact they have no clue. This assumption creates anxiety and confusion. If this fear is not addressed, it can compound other problems, and young people can become overwhelmed and discouraged. This is the point at which we most need to intervene.

An Emotional Health Curriculum

This volume in *The Passport Program* series gives educators and mental health professionals a comprehensive curriculum to help children in the elementary grades learn positive mental health concepts and navigate the journey through the situational and developmental problems of growing up. This book presents 80 activities, field tested with children in grades 1–5. These activities are designed not only to teach children what is normal, but also to help them learn effective strategies for dealing with problems characteristic of their age group. Organized by grade level, the activities cover four key areas: Self-Development, Emotional Development, Social Development, and Cognitive Development.

The activities are sequential in nature and, if used with the companion volumes for early and mid-adolescence, provide a comprehensive developmental curriculum for grades 1–12. Each activity includes a short statement about developmental perspective, specific objectives, a step-by-step lesson, and content and personalization questions. Content questions relate directly to the content of the stimulus activity and are designed to ensure mastery of concepts and processing of the stimulus activity. Personalization questions encourage children to apply the concepts to their own lives. These questions move children from intellectualizing about what they have learned to integrating the concepts personally. At the center of each activity is a creative, developmentally appropriate stimulus procedure that addresses the objectives and provides an opportunity for children to learn more about developmental issues typical for this age group, as well as to master skills for dealing with these issues. At the end of each is a follow-up activity, which reinforces the concepts in a variety of ways, including actual skill practice.

Theoretical Foundations

An important feature of this curriculum is that it is strongly grounded in developmental theory, as well as in principles of Rational-Emotive Behavior Therapy. An overview of these theories follows, but readers are encouraged to study further by consulting the references at the end of this introduction.

Developmental Characteristics: Middle Childhood

Some experts contend that middle childhood, ages 6–11, is the best period of development, in part because it is a period of relatively slow, steady growth. Middle childhood is closely associated with mastery of tasks and is called the age of *concrete operational thought,* a term that reflects the way children at this age process information. During this period of development, children gradually become less dependent on parents and channel energies into learning and discovery. Children's self-understanding expands, socialization within the context of a peer group becomes a central issue, and better problem-solving skills develop. This is a time of many "firsts": losing a tooth, staying away from home for the first time, or learning new things.

While many would contend that this period of development is the least troublesome, Elkind (1988) maintains that there is too much pressure for children to grow up "too fast, too soon" and that increasing numbers of young children experience social, emotional, and behavioral problems. Because they are somewhat limited by their ability to conceptualize and verbalize what they are experiencing, children do need support as they encounter not only the daily challenges of growing up but also more troublesome situational factors. As adults, it is sometimes easy for us to forget that a fight with a friend or anxiety about reading in front of a group is as significant as the problems and stressors we ourselves face.

Principles of Rational-Emotive Behavior Therapy

Rational-Emotive Behavior Therapy (REBT), developed by Albert Ellis (Ellis, 1994; Ellis & Dryden, 1997), is based on the assumption that what we think directly determines how we feel and behave. Ellis created the A–B–C model of emotional disturbance to explain the relationship between activating events *(A's),* beliefs *(B's),* and emotional and behavioral consequences *(C's).* According to this theory, the activating event does not create emotional upset, since two people can experience the same event and react to it differently. Rather, what we think about the event results in the emotional and behavioral reactions. Ellis maintains that disturbed, negative emotions are caused by absolutistic, rigid, and demanding thoughts, which he labeled as *irrational.* Irrational beliefs fall into three major categories: *shoulds, musts,* and *oughts,* which reflect unrealistic demands on people or situations; *evaluations of worth,* which relate to having to do well and win approval in order to consider yourself a worthwhile person; and *need statements,* which reflect what we think we must have to be comfortable and free of frustration. For children and adolescents, the *shoulds, musts,* and *oughts* translate into: I should always get to do what I want, people should treat me exactly as I think they should treat me, and everything in life should always be fair. *Evaluations of worth* translate into: I must be perfect, I can't make mistakes, and if others reject me or I don't do well, I am a worthless kid. *Need statements* reflect young people's irrational belief that everything in life should be easy: I shouldn't have to work too hard at anything or do things that are boring, and I can't stand discomfort. These irrational beliefs result in intense negative emotions, which prevent children and adolescents from engaging in effective problem solving.

For psychological health, these irrational beliefs must be replaced with *rational* beliefs. Rational beliefs result in moderate, less disturbed emotions; are based on reality; and help people achieve their goals. The process by which rational beliefs are identified is called *disputing (D)*. Disputing involves a variety of techniques for changing thinking, feeling, and behaving. Specifically, the main disputational methods include detecting illogical and unrealistic beliefs by asking questions designed to challenge these thoughts; using rational-emotive imagery; and using self-talk and self-dialogues. In addition, behavioral methods such as reinforcement, skill training, and homework assignments are widely employed.

Once irrational beliefs have been identified, the result is a reduction in the disturbing emotion. This is not to say that people go from feeling depressed to happy, or angry to slightly irritated. However, the intensity of the emotion is reduced as illogical, irrational beliefs are replaced by more sensible thoughts. For example, if a child didn't get invited to a birthday party and irrationally thought that no one liked her, that she would never have friends again, or that she was worthless because she had been rejected, she might feel very sad. If she realized through disputation that she was still a worthwhile kid even if she hadn't been invited to this party and that there was no evidence to support the fact that no one liked her or that she would never have friends again, she would still feel some sadness, but it would not be as intense. And, whereas she might have moped around for days when she was feeling very sad, she might be able to entertain herself in other ways and find some pleasure in doing those things if she were less sad. The final stages of the model, therefore, are the *E* (effective new philosophy) and *F* (new feeling).

REBT has a long history of use with children and adolescents in educational as well as therapeutic settings. The principles can be readily adapted for younger populations and have been applied to a wide variety of problems. Ellis, a long-time proponent of the use of REBT in educational settings, stresses the importance of a prevention curriculum designed to help young people help themselves by learning positive mental health concepts. Rational-Emotive Education, or REE, is a systematic curricular approach to emotional education in which planned, sequential lessons are presented. The major goal of REE is to teach rational thinking skills so children may more effectively solve problems, gain emotional insight, and learn sensible coping strategies to minimize emotional distress commonly experienced in childhood. The ultimate goal of a curriculum of this nature is to help children get better, not just feel better, and to provide them with the emotional and behavioral tools to deal more effectively with present and future problems. The activities presented in this volume are based on fundamental principles of REE and stress the application of these concepts to developmental problems.

Using Program Materials

Given the fact that growing up is more difficult than ever before, the importance of a prevention curriculum cannot be overstressed. Preventive mental health programs facilitate all aspects of development and help children develop self-acceptance, good interpersonal relationship skills, problem-solving and decision-making strategies, skills to deal with troublesome emotions, and a more flexible outlook on life. If used intentionally and sequentially, these programs can provide children with information and skills that will certainly not eliminate all problems but that can minimize the intensity, severity, and duration of problems.

The activities in this book are intended to be used primarily in classroom or small-group counseling settings. With minor changes, they can also be used in individual counseling in school or mental health settings. The developmental concepts are applicable to all children, but some adaptations of the process or the nature of the activity may need to be made for specific populations. The questions at the end of each activity are designed to stimulate discussion, and leaders are expected to expand or modify these according to the needs of the individual or group.

The stimulus activities are designed to last 20–30 minutes, followed by discussion. Obviously, this time will vary depending on the group. Some lessons may need to be divided so that the activity is completed one day, followed by discussion the next. The discussion is a critical part of these lessons because it reinforces objectives and allows children to apply the concepts to their own lives. Since many of the activities encourage self-disclosure, it is vital to establish an atmosphere of trust and cohesion prior to implementing the program. Although most of the activities are relatively nonthreatening, children must have the right to "pass" if they are uncomfortable with the discussion. Just hearing other participants share and discuss will help normalize children's feelings, and children will learn from the experience. Establishing ground rules can help ensure that children respect one another's opinions and expressions. They need to understand that these discussions are confidential and should stay within the group, that they have a right to pass, and that there should be no put-downs. Ground rules help provide children with a safe place to learn and apply these mental health principles.

As educators and mental health practitioners, we need to do what we can to safeguard children and adolescents against self-downing, irrational thinking, debilitating emotions, and self-defeating behaviors. We need to help them build resilience by teaching them how to think, feel, and behave in healthy ways. Giving them these tools should be an educational priority: It is far easier to prevent problems than to deal with them after the fact. Implementing this curriculum is a step toward facilitating children's self-, social, emotional, and cognitive development.

References and Suggested Reading

DiGiuseppe, R., & Bernard, M. (1990). The application of rational-emotive theory and therapy to school-aged children. *School Psychology Review, 19,* 287–293.

Dryden, W., & DiGiuseppe, R. (1990). *A primer on Rational-Emotive Therapy.* Champaign, IL: Research Press.

Elkind, D. (1988). *The hurried child.* Reading, MA: Addison-Wesley.

Ellis, A. (1994). *Reason and emotion in psychotherapy.* New York: Carol.

Ellis, A., & Dryden, W. (1997). *The practice of REBT.* New York: Springer.

Pipher, M. (1994). *Reviving Ophelia: Saving the selves of adolescent girls.* New York: Ballantine.

Vernon, A. (1993). *Developmental assessment and intervention with children and adolescents.* Alexandria, VA: American Counseling Association.

Vernon, A., & Al-Mabuk, R. (1995). *What growing up is all about: A parent's guide to child and adolescent development.* Champaign, IL: Research Press.

Walen, S., DiGiuseppe, R., & Dryden, W. (1992). *A practitioner's guide to Rational-Emotive Therapy.* New York: Oxford University Press.

Wilde, J. (1992). *Rational counseling with school-aged populations: A practical guide.* Muncie, IN: Accelerated Development.

the **PASSPORT** PROGRAM

Self-Development
ACTIVITY
1 I Can, They Can
2 I Like Being Me
3 I'm Growing
4 One of a Kind

Emotional Development
ACTIVITY
1 Fabulous Feelings
2 Not-So-Fabulous Feelings
3 Acting on Feelings
4 I'm Scared

Social Development
ACTIVITY
1 Building Friendships
2 Making and Keeping Friends
3 Let's Share
4 Will You Be My Friend?

Cognitive Development
ACTIVITY
1 Do I Have a Choice?
2 What's the Consequence?
3 Solutions, Solutions
4 What Should I Do?

I Can, They Can

Developmental Perspective

As children enter school, they encounter a series of new tasks. If they complete these tasks successfully, they develop a sense of mastery and achievement. If they repeatedly fail, they develop feelings of inadequacy and incompetence. Because they are routinely around peers in a learning environment, they begin to compare themselves to others and make judgments about their abilities and behavior in relation to others. This information is incorporated into their self-concept. It is therefore important for children at this age to realize that everyone has strengths and weaknesses and, although there are always things others may be able to do better than they can, that doesn't mean they are incompetent or worthless.

Objectives

▷ To learn that everyone has strengths and weaknesses

▷ To learn that everyone is worthwhile regardless of weaknesses

Materials

▷ Chalkboard

▷ Two building blocks or bricks

▷ A low table that a child would have to crawl under

▷ Something heavy, such as a bucket filled with sand, that could be lifted only by a stronger child

▷ A jump rope

▷ A set of jacks

▷ Several spelling words that would be too difficult for a first grader to spell

▷ Several math problems that would be too difficult for a first grader to do

▷ Paper and crayons for each child (for the Follow-up Activity)

Procedure

1. Prior to the activity, arrange the room as follows:

   ► Place the blocks or bricks on a shelf so high it will take a tall child to reach them.

   ► Arrange the table so it is in a small space and only a small child can crawl underneath it.

   ► Have the other materials available.

2. Introduce this lesson by asking children to raise their hands if they can do the following:

   ► Walk on water

   ► Fly like a bird

   ► Run fast

   ► Spell words

   ► Be kind to others

   ► Climb a mountain

3. Emphasize that there are some things that everyone can do, some things that no one can do, and some things that some people can do and others can't. Tell children that you are going to be asking for several volunteers to help you with some tasks. These tasks will show that people have certain strengths, or things they can do, as well as certain weaknesses, or things they can't do.

4. For the first task, invite a short child and a tall child to reach for the blocks or bricks. Ask children to observe what happens. Before proceeding to the second task, briefly discuss the results and record them on the chalkboard. (Follow this recording procedure for the rest of the tasks.) For the second task, invite a larger child and a smaller one to crawl under the table. For the third, invite a smaller child and a larger child to lift the heavy object. For the jump rope and jacks, invite both a boy and a girl to use these objects. For the spelling words, invite two good spellers. For the math problems, invite two good math students.

5. Process the activity by asking the Content and Personalization Questions.

Discussion

Content Questions

Leader note: Refer to the information recorded on the chalkboard after each task was completed.

1. What happened when two children reached for the bricks or blocks? Could they do it equally as easily? If not, why?

2. What happened when two children crawled under the table? Could they do this equally as easily? Why or why not?

3. What happened when two children lifted the heavy object? Was it equally easy or difficult? Why or why not?

4. What happened when two children tried to spell the words or do the math problems? Was it easy for both of them? If not, why do you think it wasn't?

5. What happened when two children tried to jump rope or play jacks? Was it easy for both of them? If not, why do you think it wasn't?

6. Do you think it is possible for everybody to do everything equally well? Does it mean you are no good if there are some things that others can do better than you?

7. Suppose you couldn't do any of these tasks. Would this mean you were a "no good" kid? What would it mean?

PERSONALIZATION QUESTIONS

1. Have you ever thought that other students in your class or other people in your family could do things better than you could? If they could, why do you suppose they were able to do this? Do you think that all children should be able to do everything equally well?

2. If you can't do something as well as one of your classmates or your brother or sister, should you think of yourself as dumb, stupid, weak, or bad?

3. What can you tell yourself the next time you start to think you are no good because you can't do something?

Follow-up Activity

Invite children to interview parents or grandparents to see if they think children should be able to do everything everyone else can. As an alternate activity, have children divide a sheet of paper in half. On one side, have them draw a picture of something they can do, and on the other side, a picture of something they can't do.

I Like Being Me

Developmental Perspective

As children begin to expand their level of self-awareness and compare their abilities to those of their peers, they may experience feelings of incompetence or dissatisfaction, which can negatively affect their concept of themselves. Helping them learn to accept themselves is very important at this stage of development.

Objectives

▷ To identify what children like about being who they are

▷ To develop an attitude of self-acceptance

Materials

▷ None

Procedure

1. Introduce the lesson by asking children to raise their hands if they have ever pretended they have been someone else or wished they were different than how they really are. Invite sharing about this.

2. Tell children you will be reading a story about a boy who wanted to be different. However, when he changed, he didn't like that either. After a while, he learned to appreciate himself for who he was.

3. Read the following story aloud to the children, then discuss the Content and Personalization Questions.

GEORGE'S CHAMELEON
by David Martino

George was riding the bus home from school, looking at his reflection in the window, thinking about his day, and feeling pretty sad. "I just don't fit in," thought George. "Everybody can do something special except me." He got off the bus, and as he was kicking a rock in front of him, he thought, "Jimmy is great at soccer, Sarah is a braniac at math, Pete draws great comic strips, and here I am—I can't do anything. I wish I could be like them. But instead, I'm just good old George; that's what they say, good old George, like I'm a dog or something."

When George walked through the door of his house, he nearly jumped out of his skin at the big "Surprise!" he heard. He had almost forgotten that today was his birthday! His mom, dad, big brother, and little sister were standing in front of some presents arranged on the dinner table. George secretly hoped that one of the presents was what he'd been asking for all these months. "Go ahead, open 'em," said George's dad, and George tore in. One baseball mitt, a comic book, and a pair of jeans later, the present George had hoped for was nowhere to be found. George forced a smile and said, "This is really nice," as his mother reached behind the couch and said, "There's one more, George." She picked up a cage and handed it to George. Inside the cage was what George had asked for all these months—a chameleon! "I have no idea why you wanted a chameleon, Georgie," said his mother. "But here you go—happy birthday!"

George was overjoyed. Ever since he had checked out a book on chameleons from the library, he had developed a real interest and fascination with the animal. What George especially liked was how the chameleon could change its skin color to blend in with its surroundings. Sure enough, when George changed the background on the cage from blue to black, the chameleon changed its skin from blue to black. When he changed it to a spotted background, the chameleon had spotted skin, too. George was amazed.

George took his chameleon, whom he named Cammi, up to his bedroom. George continued to watch Cammi change colors. Immediately after his dinner, homework, and bath, George went straight to his room to play with Cammi some more. When his father came to check on George that night, he found that George had fallen asleep in front of Cammi's cage. His father lifted George into bed and covered him up.

That night, George had a dream. He dreamed he was at school. The dream began with George out on the playground before the morning bell. But then he watched himself do something very strange. When he got close to his friend Jimmy, who was built sort of tall and stocky, George felt his own body grow until it was just the same as Jimmy's body. Not only that, but the clothes that George was wearing slowly changed so that they matched exactly what Jimmy was wearing. And, in fact, George's face even began to look like Jimmy's face. It was kind of nice at first—he had always admired how Jimmy looked. George found that he could play soccer better than he had ever played before, but he was also a little scared because nobody seemed to recognize him. His friend Brett looked right at him and asked, "Where's George?"

Before George could answer, in his dream the bell rang, and the children went inside. George sat at his desk, right next to Sarah. The same thing started to happen again. His body, his clothes, and finally his face looked just like Sarah's. He looked at his math problems, and the questions that used to be a struggle for him were now very easy. But again, it upset him that behind all the changes, no one seemed to know who he was. Everyone looked at him like he was just another Sarah instead of seeing the same old George underneath. George went to sharpen his pencil and met up with Pete. Instantly, George's body, clothes, and face started to change to match Pete's. He sharpened his pencil, then drew a fantastic picture of a flying elephant, better than he had ever drawn before. Elizabeth came over to look at George's picture and said, "Nice picture, Pete!"

George got more and more scared because no matter what he tried, it seemed he couldn't convince anybody that he was just plain old George. He approached his friends, but then he would just change and change. He changed so much that he got a little panicky, and he began to wish that he hadn't wished to be like somebody else. "I'm me!" George cried, "I'm me!" His classmates just looked at him with confusion on their faces. George put his head in his hands and sobbed, "I just wish I was me, just plain old George, George, George . . ."

"George, George, Georgie," said his mother as she gently shook him. "Wake up, sleepy-head, time for school."

"Mom?" said George.

"You were tossing and turning all over the place, Georgie. Were you having a bad dream?"

"Yeah, Mom."

"Well, it's over now. Time to get up. And don't forget to feed Cammi."

George climbed out of bed, and he was a little shaken because the dream had seemed so real. George looked at Cammi, who was sitting languidly in his cage, fading into the background as always. George could swear that Cammi winked at him.

When George arrived at school, he had to check twice to make sure that his body, clothes, or face wasn't changing. He got to his desk and lost himself in thought about the dream he had had the night before. Sarah leaned over and said, "Hey, George, whatcha dreaming about?"

"What did you call me?" asked George.

"Why, George, of course," replied Sarah. "That's your name, isn't it?"

"That's right," said George. "That's me." And he smiled at how happy he felt just to be himself.

Discussion

CONTENT QUESTIONS

1. Why did George want to be different?

2. Why did George think there wasn't anything special about him?

3. How did George feel about the way he changed in his dream?

4. By the end of the story, was George glad to be who he was?
   If so, why do you think he changed his mind?

PERSONALIZATION QUESTIONS

1. Have you ever wished that you could be different? If so, how would you like to be different?

2. What do you like about the way you are?

3. Even if there are some things about you that you might like to change, can you accept yourself just as you are? Are you, like George, glad to be you?

Follow-up Activity

Have children make up a song entitled "What I Like about Me." Allow time for them to sing their song to the other children. Having pots, pans, drums, triangles, and other objects to use as musical instruments may enhance their creativity.

I'm Growing

Developmental Perspective

Losing teeth is one of the most significant physical changes that occurs during this period of development, but in addition there are gradual significant changes in height, weight, and strength. Muscular control also continues to develop, and although children's control of their large muscles is considerably better than control of their smaller muscles, small muscle control gradually begins to improve. Locomotor skills, agility, and coordination also become better developed as children mature.

Objectives

▷ To identify ways in which children are physically growing and changing

▷ To identify competencies associated with physical changes

Materials

▷ Three pictures that each child brings from home
(age 0–2, age 3–4, and age 5–present)

▷ A copy of the I'm Growing–Worksheet (Handout 1) for each child

▷ A sheet of white drawing paper, a pencil, and crayons for each child

Procedure

1. Invite children to take out the pictures they brought for this activity. Distribute a copy of the I'm Growing–Worksheet (Handout 1) to each child.

2. Next review the categories on the chart with the children: teeth, hair, size of feet, size of hands, height, weight, and overall appearance. Explain the meaning of the words *same* and *different,* and indicate that children will be examining their pictures and circling the word *same* or *different* as you lead them through the activity.

3. First have children compare their baby picture to the picture of themselves at age 3–4. Read each of the categories on the chart and have children circle the word *same* or *different* as it applies to each category. Then follow the same procedure for the comparison of ages 3–4 and 5–present.

4. When they have finished completing the chart, discuss the Content Questions. Then distribute drawing paper and crayons and ask children to draw a picture of something they could do at age 3–4 that they couldn't do during infancy. On the reverse side, ask them to draw a picture of something they can now do that they couldn't do at age 3–4.

5. Discuss the Personalization Questions.

Discussion

CONTENT QUESTIONS

1. In looking at what you circled on your chart for the 0–2 and the 3–4 age categories, did you have more that were the same or more that were different? What about for the 3–4 and 5–present comparison?

2. Based on your chartings, what have you learned about how you have changed?

PERSONALIZATION QUESTIONS

1. What is something you can do now that you couldn't do when you were between the ages of 3 and 4? What is something you could do when you were between 3 and 4 that you couldn't do when you were a baby?

2. Can you think of anything you can't do now that you could do when you were between the ages of 3 and 4?

3. Are you happy about the fact that you are growing and changing? What do you like best about being your present age?

Follow-up Activity

Display the pictures in the room. In a large group, invite children to select one of their pictures and tell two things they remember about themselves at that age.

I'm Growing

WORKSHEET

Name: _____ Date: _____

	Age 0–2 to 3–4	Age 3–4 to 5–present
Teeth	Same Different	Same Different
Hair	Same Different	Same Different
Feet	Same Different	Same Different
Hands	Same Different	Same Different
Height	Same Different	Same Different
Weight	Same Different	Same Different
Overall appearance	Same Different	Same Different

One of a Kind

Developmental Perspective

Children's growing awareness of themselves during this period is critical in terms of their overall self-development. Because far too many children live in homes where there is very little nurturance, positive reinforcement, or support, it is important to help children recognize the particular ways in which they are special.

Objectives

▷ To identify ways each child is special

▷ To recognize one's own uniqueness

Materials

▷ A rubber stamp pad and several magnifying glasses

▷ A copy of the One of a Kind–Worksheet (Handout 2) for each child

▷ A small paper plate, safety pin, and crayons for each child
   (for the Follow-up Activity)

Procedure

1. Introduce this lesson by having children close their eyes and imagine they are going to the toy store. While they are there, they are going to be looking for a toy that is "one of a kind." Ask them what it means to find something that is one of a kind. Elicit suggestions, reinforcing the idea that this means there is something special or different about this toy. Indicate that children are like that, too; there is usually something special about them that is not exactly like anyone else.

2. Distribute copies of the One of a Kind–Worksheet (Handout 2). Next pass around the stamp pad and have children press their thumbs into the pad and put their thumbprints on the top of the worksheet.

3. When this has been completed, have each child find a partner and compare thumbprints to discover whether or not they are exactly alike (using the magnifying glasses will facilitate this). After some discussion of the fact that no two thumbprints are exactly alike–that every child's is unique–refer again to the worksheet. Read each of the phrases aloud, then have children draw a picture to illustrate their responses.

4. After the worksheet has been completed, invite sharing of responses so children can learn more about the ways in which they are like as well as unlike others.

5. Process the activity by discussing the Content and Personalization Questions.

Discussion

CONTENT QUESTIONS

1. What did you see when you compared your thumbprint to your partner's print? In what ways were your thumbprints different?

2. When you listened to others share their answers to the questions on the worksheet, could you identify ways in which you are like others? Unlike others?

PERSONALIZATION QUESTIONS

1. Think of yourself as the special toy in the toy store. How are you special or different from other toys in this group?

2. What do you like best about yourself?

Follow-up Activity

Invite children to make a "One of a Kind" badge by using a small paper plate. Have them draw things on the badge that illustrate how they think they are special. They can pin the completed badges to their shirts.

One of a Kind

WORKSHEET

Name: _____ Date: _____

MY THUMBPRINT

Something I do to help my family is: _____

_____

Something I do to help my teacher is: _____

_____

Something I can do well is: _____

_____

Fabulous Feelings

Developmental Perspective

Middle childhood has often been described as the "best years" of a child's life. Growth is slower during this period of development, and children are exposed to many new and exciting experiences: walking alone to Grandma's for the first time, learning to ride a bike, or joining after-school clubs. Despite the fact that some of these new experiences can create anxiety and uncertainty, there are many positive feelings associated with this period of development if it is not overshadowed by situational stressors.

Objectives

▷ To identify positive feelings

▷ To develop a feelings vocabulary

Materials

▷ Chalkboard

▷ A one-quart milk carton per child, cut in half. Use the bottom half for the activity. (Children could bring their own, or you could use library pocket envelopes if it is too difficult to get milk cartons.)

▷ One set of Fabulous Feelings–Cards (Handout 3), in an envelope, for each child

Procedure

1. Discuss the difference between positive feelings, which we like to have, and negative feelings, which we don't like to have. Ask children to give some examples of each.

2. Distribute the milk cartons and envelopes of Fabulous Feelings–Cards (Handout 3). As you discuss the meanings of the words in the envelope, write them on the chalkboard so children will be able to recognize them when they are asked to select a word to describe how they would feel about a particular event.

3. Read the first two of the following scenarios and have children select words to describe how they would feel about each of these situations. Have them put the words in their cartons. Ask several volunteers to share the words they selected.

   FABULOUS FEELINGS SCENARIOS

   ► You haven't seen your grandparents for a long time. Your dad tells you they are coming for a visit.

   ► Your birthday is next week, and you are having some friends over for a party.

▶ You just got your math paper back, and you got all the problems right.

▶ You just took a bath, and your older sister read you a story before bedtime.

▶ You have wanted a kitten for a long time. Today your mom is going to take you to the Humane Society to pick one out.

▶ You just baked your first cake.

▶ You are going to walk to school tomorrow with two of your very good friends.

▶ Your cousins are coming over to play.

▶ Your new baby sister is coming home from the hospital tomorrow.

▶ You figured out how to spell some hard words.

4. Continue this procedure, reading two scenarios at a time, until all have been read and the feelings shared. Then discuss the Content and Personalization Questions.

Discussion

CONTENT QUESTIONS

1. Did everyone select the same feeling word for each situation? If not, why do you suppose this happened?

2. Do you think that more than one feeling could be used to describe some of the situations? If so, give some examples.

PERSONALIZATION QUESTIONS

1. Have you experienced positive feelings like the ones described in this activity?

2. Can you share examples of times you have had good feelings like these?

3. What do you think you can do to keep experiencing good feelings?

Follow-up Activity

Invite children to keep their cartons on their desks or at home in their rooms. They can drop a feeling word in the carton whenever they experience something positive. At the end of the day, they can share these positive feelings with a teacher, parent, or sibling.

Fabulous Feelings

CARDS

Leader note: Each set should contain the following words: proud *(three cards),* happy *(three cards),* excited *(three cards),* calm *(two cards),* cheerful *(two cards), and* wonderful *(two cards).*

Proud	Proud	Proud
Happy	Happy	Happy
Excited	Excited	Excited
Calm	Calm	Calm
Cheerful	Cheerful	Cheerful
Wonderful	Wonderful	Wonderful

Not-So-Fabulous Feelings

Developmental Perspective

Along with the fabulous feelings associated with the many firsts of middle childhood, there can be negative feelings: uncertainty about doing something new, anxiety associated with school performance, or fear about leaving the security of the family to spend more time with friends. Certainly these negative feelings increase if there are situational factors such as changing family circumstances, abuse, or parental alcoholism. Developmentally, children at this age may have difficulty verbalizing feelings because they don't have the feelings vocabulary, but they are becoming more perceptive about their own as well as others' feelings.

Objectives

▷ To identify negative feelings

▷ To develop a feelings vocabulary

Materials

▷ Chalkboard

▷ A one-quart milk carton per child, cut in half. Use the bottom half for the activity. (Children could bring their own, or you could use library pocket cards if it is too difficult to get milk cartons.)

▷ One set of Not-So-Fabulous Feelings–Cards (Handout 4), in an envelope, for each child

Procedure

1. Discuss the difference between the positive (fabulous) feelings identified in the previous activity and negative feelings: feelings we don't like to have because we don't feel good when we have them. Ask children to identify some examples of these negative feelings.

2. Distribute the milk cartons and envelopes of Not-So-Fabulous Feelings–Cards (Handout 4). As you discuss the meanings of the words in the envelope, write them on the chalkboard so children will be able to recognize them when they are asked to select a word to describe how they feel about a particular event.

3. Read the first two of the following scenarios and have children select words to describe how they would feel about each of these situations. Have them put the words in their cartons, then ask several volunteers to share the words they selected. (If they would have a positive feeling about the situation, they do not select a word from their envelope to put in the carton.)

NOT-SO-FABULOUS FEELINGS SCENARIOS

► You are outside for recess, and one of your friends makes fun of you because you didn't run very fast.

► You are at the market with your mother. She buys your sister some candy and won't buy any for you.

► You are taking swimming lessons because you don't know how to swim. Tomorrow is your first lesson.

► You got your reading worksheet back. You didn't get very many right.

► Your brother takes your rollerblades without asking if he can use them.

► Your dad is in jail for selling drugs.

► You are moving to a new neighborhood. You have to say good-bye to all your good friends.

► You are riding the school bus for the first time.

► Your mom and dad are getting a divorce.

► Your new baby brother is getting all of your parents' and grandparents' attention.

4. Continue this procedure, reading two scenarios at a time, until all have been read and the feelings shared. Then discuss the Content and Personalization Questions.

Discussion

CONTENT QUESTIONS

1. Did everyone select the same feeling word for each situation? If not, why do you think this happened?

2. Do you think that more than one feeling could be used to describe some of the situations? If so, give some examples.

PERSONALIZATION QUESTIONS

1. Have you ever experienced negative feelings like the ones identified in this activity?

2. Can you share examples of times you have had some of these negative feelings?

3. If you have negative feelings, what are some things you can do to help yourself feel better?

Leader note: Make a list of children's suggestions and post them in the room so children can refer to them as needed.

Follow-up Activity

Invite children to keep their cartons on their desks or at home in their rooms. They can drop a feeling word in the carton when they experience something negative. At the end of the day, they can share these negative feelings with a teacher, parent, or sibling.

Not-So-Fabulous Feelings

CARDS

Leader note: Each set should contain the following words: mad *(three cards),* scared *(three cards),* jealous *(two cards),* worried *(two cards),* furious *(two cards), and* sad *(two cards).*

Mad	Mad	Mad
Scared	Scared	Scared
Jealous	Jealous	Jealous
Worried	Worried	Worried
Furious	Furious	Furious
Sad	Sad	Sad

Acting on Feelings

Developmental Perspective

Children need to learn that there is a relationship between how they feel and how they act. They also need to learn that it is good to express feelings, but the way they express them can have a positive or a negative impact. Learning appropriate ways to express negative feelings is an important skill at this stage of development.

Objectives

▷ To learn the connection between feelings and behaviors

▷ To identify appropriate ways to express negative feelings

Materials

▷ Chalkboard

▷ Two puppets

▷ Videotaped children's cartoons (for the Follow-up Activity)

Procedure

1. Ask for two volunteers who will assume the roles of the puppets.
2. Take the volunteers aside and read them the first of the following scenarios. Instruct them that they are to act out the scenario for the other students. As an alternative, you could act out the scenario with the puppets instead of using volunteers.

ACTING ON FEELINGS SCENARIOS

► It's your birthday, and your aunt gives you a new shirt. You think it is really ugly. You don't say anything; you just make a "yucky" face and stuff it back in the box.

► One of the kids in your neighborhood invites you over for supper. His parents fix macaroni, which you hate. When the meal is served you ask them if there is anything else to eat because you can't stand this food.

► You are at school, and one of your classmates has volunteered to read her story out loud to the class. You think the story is really stupid. When she is finished, everyone but you claps and tells her she did a good job.

► A boy in your neighborhood just got a new bike. He is really excited about it. Your parents couldn't afford to buy you a new bike, so they got a used one for you. You are jealous of this boy's new bike, but you don't want him to know it. You tell him his bike is an ugly color and you bet it won't go as fast as your bike.

► You have been playing baseball in the neighborhood. When it is your turn at bat, you strike out. Another kid makes fun of you. You are angry, so you punch him out.

3. After the volunteers have enacted the first scenario, elicit the following from the rest of the students:

► Were the feelings expressed positive or negative? How could you tell?

► What was the consequence of the way the first puppet expressed feelings to the second puppet?

► What could have been done differently to change this consequence from a bad one to a better one?

Ask two new volunteers to show what could have been done differently to change the consequence from a bad one to a better one. An alternative would be for children to come up one at a time and give the puppets suggestions for more appropriate ways to handle the situation.

4. Continue with the remaining scenarios, following the procedures described, then discuss the Content and Personalization Questions.

Discussion

Content Questions

1. How do you think the way you feel affects the way you act?

2. Which do you think was the best way to express feelings: the first or the second? Why do you think this?

3. What were the differences between the first and the second ways of acting on the feelings?

Leader note: Write the differences suggested on the chalkboard and discuss.

Personalization Questions

1. If you are happy, how do you act on that feeling? If you are sad, how do you act? If you are angry, how do you act? If you are worried or afraid, how do you act?

2. If you don't act in a way that produces positive results, what are some ways you could change this?

Follow-up Activity

Show the videotaped cartoons and ask children to watch for how the cartoon characters act, how they might be feeling, and what effect their actions might have on others.

I'm Scared

Developmental Perspective

A vivid imagination is characteristic of this age level. Given that 5- and 6-year-olds still sometimes have difficulty distinguishing between fantasy and reality, it is not uncommon for them to be afraid of the dark, imagining that monsters will attack them as they sleep. This fear may also generalize to the "bogeymen" they are convinced are hiding in the yard, ready to grab them. Generally, by the end of first grade children have outgrown this fear, but until that time the fear is very genuine and affects their ability to sleep or, in some cases, go outside to play. Children need to know that although their fears are normal, there are things they can do to empower themselves to overcome these fears.

Objective

▷ To develop coping strategies to deal with normal fears

Materials

▷ One empty aerosol can per child (for the Follow-up Activity).
   (Ask children to bring a can from home, or draw a picture of a can
   and duplicate it if cans are not available.)

▷ Construction paper, glue, and markers or crayons for each child
   (for the Follow-up Activity)

Procedure

1. Introduce the activity by explaining that many children are afraid of such things as monsters or bogeymen. Indicate that while it is normal to feel afraid, it is also possible to do something about these fears, as the story you will read illustrates.

2. Read the following story aloud to the children, then discuss the Content and Personalization Questions.

I'M SCARED

It was the summer before first grade, and Jason had just moved to a new neighborhood. He was really happy about that because there were lots of kids his age in the block. He and his sister had a big back yard to play in, and his parents had built them a tree house. The only problem was that Jason was afraid to go outside alone. At first his dad thought it was because he was new in the neighborhood and was afraid he would get lost, but Jason knew that wasn't the reason. He knew his way around, and if his friends were outside, he felt all right. The problem was this: Jason was afraid that a bogeyman would come and get him if he was outside alone and there was no one there to protect him. He really didn't want to tell anyone because he thought they might make fun of him. His grandparents were always saying what a "big boy" he was, and he figured that big boys shouldn't be afraid of things like bogeymen. His friends didn't seem like they were afraid, and even his sister, who was a year younger, wasn't afraid. Jason didn't know what to do.

One day when Jason's sister was gone and none of his friends was outside, Jason was watching television. His mom came in and said, "Jason, it's a perfectly nice day. You should be outside playing." "I just want to finish this show and then I'll go," Jason said. But as he was watching the show, he started getting a little stomachache because he was worried about going out alone.

When the show ended, his mom came back in. "Mom, I can't go outside because I have a stomachache. Maybe I'll just stay inside and play," Jason said. Jason's mom just looked at him and said, "Jason, I think you might be afraid to go outside alone since there is nobody around. I bet if you could tell me what you are afraid of, we could figure out something to help you so you wouldn't have to be afraid."

So Jason told her. His mom didn't laugh or tell him to be brave like he thought she might. Instead, she said, "When I was your age, I was afraid to go to bed because I thought a monster would come out from under my bed and get me. I think I understand a little bit about what you might be feeling. Let's see if we can think of some things that might help you feel safer when you go outside."

Jason and his mom both put their thinking caps on. They thought and thought. Pretty soon Jason had an idea! He told his mom that maybe he could make a scary mask and hang it in the yard. That way the bogeyman would be afraid to come into the yard. His mom thought that was a fantastic idea. She asked him what else he could try, and he came up with the idea of making some "bogeyman spray" that he could spray in the yard before he went out to play. He said that might keep the bogeyman away just like bug spray keeps bugs away.

His mom really liked that idea, too. "Jason, I think you'd better get started making that mask and the bogeyman spray." So off Jason went. As soon as he was finished, he and his mom hung up the mask and sprayed the yard. He was still a little afraid, so his mom suggested that he try going out for a few minutes at a time. Then if nothing scary happened, he could tell himself that since everything went fine for 10 minutes, why not try 10 more?

Jason decided that was a good idea and went out to his tree house. He felt a lot better, knowing that the mask was up and that he had used his bogeyman spray. He got busy in the tree house, and before he knew it, his dad called him in for lunch. He had completely forgotten about the time and had been outside, alone, for almost an hour without feeling scared! When he finished lunch, he thought to himself, "Nothing scary happened to me when I was out before, so I can try this again and not be scared."

Discussion

CONTENT QUESTIONS

1. Do you think Jason will be afraid to go out in the yard again? Why or why not?
2. Why was Jason afraid to tell his parents and his friends why he didn't want to go outside?
3. What helped Jason feel less afraid?

PERSONALIZATION QUESTIONS

1. Have you ever had a fear like Jason or his mother had?
2. What did you do to help yourself get over the fear?
3. What did you learn from this story that might help you if you have fears like Jason or his mother had?

Follow-up Activity

Distribute the aerosol cans and have children make their own "monster spray" by covering the can with paper and decorating it. Making masks to scare away the monsters or bogeymen would be an alternate activity.

Building Friendships

Developmental Perspective

Peer relationships serve an important function for children. As they interact with others, children learn about values, behaviors, and beliefs that will help them become functioning members of society. Because friendships play an increasingly significant role in their lives, learning how to develop good relationships is a vital part of social development.

Objective

▷ To identify ways to develop good relationships with others

Materials

▷ Two sheets of paper and crayons for each child

▷ A roll of masking tape

Procedure

1. Ask children to raise their hands if they have ever seen a brick wall or a brick building. Discuss the fact that in building a wall or a building, a lot of individual bricks are put together. Explain that in this lesson they will be building a "wall of friendship."

2. Give each child a sheet of paper and explain that this is each child's "brick." Then ask them to take out crayons and draw a picture (with the paper placed horizontally) to illustrate one of the following:

   ► How to invite someone to play

   ► How to cooperate or share with a friend

   ► How to let someone know you'd like to be his or her friend

   ► Something nice you can do for a friend

3. After children have finished drawing, invite them, one at a time, to share their friendship bricks. Tape the bricks up to form the wall of friendship.

4. Process the activity by discussing the Content and Personalization Questions.

Discussion

CONTENT QUESTIONS

1. Did the picture you drew show something you have done in a friendship situation?

2. Are there other ways of building friendships that weren't shown in the pictures drawn for this lesson? (Invite sharing of examples.)

3. What are some things you think don't help in building friendships? (Examples include hitting, refusing to share, and so forth. Stress that children should not use names when giving examples.)

PERSONALIZATION QUESTIONS

1. What is one thing you do that shows that you are a good friend to others?

2. Did you learn some new things about building friendships from other children's drawings? If so, what did you learn?

3. Which ideas would you like to try to help you be a better friend?

Follow-up Activity

Have children draw more pictures of positive friendship behaviors and add these "bricks" to the friendship wall.

Making & Keeping Friends

Developmental Perspective

Many changes occur during middle childhood with regard to social development. As children get older, they gradually expand their friendship circles and therefore need to develop skills to help them make and keep friends. At this particular age they are becoming less egocentric and can understand concepts such as "give and take." They are becoming more skilled at cooperation and sharing, and are better able to interpret social cues. However, these skills need to be continually reinforced. Since quarreling, insults, and derogatory remarks increase at this age, emphasis on the negative impact of these behaviors is also important for social development.

Objectives

▷ To differentiate between behaviors that do and do not contribute to making and keeping friends

▷ To identify effective ways to deal with peers who demonstrate negative friendship behaviors

Materials

▷ Chalkboard

▷ Chairs, paper plates, or carpet squares

▷ An audiotape player and a taped children's song

▷ A sheet of newsprint and a marker

▷ A large paper bag

▷ Crayons and several sheets of paper, folded and stapled together to form a book (one per child; for the Follow-up Activity)

Procedure

1. Introduce the lesson by asking children to raise a hand if they:

    ► Like it when a friend calls them a name

    ► Like it when a friend shares with them

    ► Like it when a friend argues with them

    ► Like it when a friend invites them to play

    Briefly discuss their responses and indicate that the purpose of this lesson is to identify behaviors that can help them make and keep friends.

2. Ask children to bring a chair to the front of the room. (If space is limited or chairs are attached to desks, they could use paper plates or carpet squares.) They should place the chairs in a big circle and then sit down. When everyone is seated, explain that they will be playing a game similar to musical chairs and that, first, you will take one of the chairs out of the circle. Next you will play some music. When the music stops, children are to sit down on the chairs. The child left standing will respond to one of the following items. This child must state whether he or she thinks this is a good way or a bad way to make and keep a friend. Before starting the music again, ask the rest of the children if they agree with the response. If not, discuss and arrive at a consensus before moving on. Then have the standing child rejoin the circle as the others stand up and move once again to the music. When the music stops, the child left standing responds to the next item, and so on until all items have been read.

- ► Teases you
- ► Ignores you
- ► Shares with you
- ► Calls you a name
- ► Gives you a hug
- ► Sticks out his or her tongue at you
- ► Tells you a funny joke
- ► Cuts in front of you in line
- ► Won't let you play
- ► Makes fun of your clothes
- ► Invites you to play
- ► Tattles on you
- ► Invites you to sit by him or her at lunch
- ► Lies to you
- ► Tells you that you are fun to work with on an assignment
- ► Tells you you're smart
- ► Tells you what you are wearing looks nice
- ► Pushes you
- ► Threatens to beat you up
- ► Takes turns doing things with you
- ► Lets you play with something very special
- ► Trips you

3. Next list the following on the chalkboard:

> ► Teases you
>
> ► Sticks out his or her tongue at you
>
> ► Ignores you
>
> ► Calls you a name
>
> ► Tattles on you

Ask children how they feel when these things happen to them. Discuss how they usually handle these kinds of situations and how well these methods work, differentiating between positive and negative ways of responding. As children share, list the positive suggestions on a sheet of newsprint and post so they can refer to them as needed.

4. Next take out the paper bag and place it over your head. Ask children if they think you can see anything when you are wearing this bag. Then tell them that since there are no ears on the bag, you also can't hear anything. Ask for five volunteers. Have each volunteer choose one of the negative behaviors previously listed on the chalkboard and do it to you, one at a time. As they do so, remain silent and do not react. When all five have finished, take off the bag and discuss the Content and Personalization Questions.

Discussion

CONTENT QUESTIONS

1. What happened when I put the paper bag over my head? Could I see what others were doing? Could I hear what they were saying? (Remember, there weren't any "ears" on the bag.)

2. Did I react to anything the volunteers said or did? Suppose this happened in real life–someone called you a name and you just pretended that you had a paper bag over your head and didn't hear it. What do you suppose would happen? Suppose someone made a face at you and you pretended you had a bag over your head and didn't see it. What do you suppose would happen?

3. Do you think you can stop others from calling you names, teasing you, or doing some of the other negative friendship behaviors identified during the game? Just because people do these things, do you have to get upset? Do you think it helps to get sad or angry when others treat you like this?

PERSONALIZATION QUESTIONS

1. Have you been in a situation where others have used some of the negative friendship behaviors discussed in this lesson?

2. If this has happened to you, have you used some of the techniques suggested during the discussion? How have they worked for you?

3. What did you learn in this lesson that will help you make and keep friends?

4. What is something you can do when others use negative friendship behaviors with you?

Follow-up Activity

Distribute the stapled paper "books." Have children draw pictures during the week to illustrate things they do to make and keep friends. Allow time for them to share these with the group.

Let's Share

Developmental Perspective

By age 7, children are beginning to outgrow their egocentrism and are demonstrating more prosocial skills, such as sharing and showing concern for others. However, because children develop at different rates, lessons in sharing facilitate this skill development.

Objective

▷ To develop skills in sharing

Materials

▷ A lunch-size paper bag, yarn, and fabric or wallpaper scraps for each partnership

▷ Crayons, scissors, and glue for each partnership

▷ A newsprint version of the Let's Share–Chart (Handout 5; for the Follow-up Activity)

Procedure

1. Introduce the lesson by asking children what it means to share. Elicit examples of sharing.

2. Ask each child to find a partner. Give each partnership a paper bag, yarn, fabric or wallpaper scraps, crayons, scissors, and glue. Instruct them to use these materials to make one puppet.

3. When they have finished making the puppets, have each set of partners join another set of partners. As a group of four, they should make up a short play about some aspect of friendship, using their two puppets. Allow time for children to present their puppet plays to the rest of the group.

Discussion

CONTENT QUESTIONS

1. Did you and your partner have any difficulty sharing the materials and ideas to make the puppet?

2. How did you share? Were there certain things you said or did?

3. What does it mean to share?

PERSONALIZATION QUESTIONS

1. Do you and your friends share with each other?

2. If you have brothers and sisters, do you share with them?

3. What is the most difficult thing about sharing?

4. Do you think it is important to share? How do you feel when others don't share with you?

Follow-up Activity

Post the newsprint version of the Let's Share–Chart (Handout 5). At the end of each day for a week, spend several minutes eliciting ideas from the children about the ways they shared with each other or their siblings or neighborhood friends. List their responses on the chart and keep it posted in the room so children can refer to it and continue to practice various ways of sharing.

Let's Share

CHART

	With friends at school	With brothers/sisters	With neighbors
Monday			
Tuesday			
Wednesday			
Thursday			
Friday			

Will You Be My Friend?

Developmental Perspective

Because friendships are beginning to play an increasingly important role, it is important to help children develop skills that will enhance their interpersonal relationships. By understanding the differences between positive and negative friendship behaviors, children will have more knowledge to apply in social interactions.

Objective

▷ To distinguish between positive and negative friendship behaviors

Materials

▷ Chalkboard

▷ Two puppets

Procedure

1. Introduce the lesson by acting out a short scenario with two puppets to illustrate negative ways of interacting with others (shoving, pushing, not sharing, and so on). After this brief demonstration, ask children if they would want to play with these puppets, and, if not, why not? What didn't they like about the way these two puppets played together?

2. Next invite two students to use the puppets to demonstrate better ways to play. After they have finished, discuss the differences between the two puppet plays and help children clearly identify positive versus negative friendship behaviors (list these on the chalkboard).

3. Read the following story to the children, then discuss the Content and Personalization Questions.

WILL YOU BE MY FRIEND?

Friendly Frieda had been roaming the neighborhood all morning looking for someone to play with. She couldn't figure out where everyone was. Finally, she saw Rude Rachael sitting on her front step. Frieda skipped across the yard and said, "Hi, Rachael! I've been looking everywhere for someone to play with. Do you want to do something together?" Rachael didn't bother to answer, so Frieda zoomed in a little closer, thinking that perhaps Rachael hadn't heard her. She tried again: "Rachael, I was wondering if you'd like to come over to my house or do something in the neighborhood together?"

Rude Rachael glared at Friendly Frieda and mumbled, "I don't want to play with you. Just get out of my yard." Frieda was shocked. "Rachael, I don't understand. The last time we played together I thought we had fun. I even let you use my new rollerblades."

Rachael stuck out her tongue at Frieda and made a face. "Well, I didn't have fun, and I don't want to play with you. Just leave me alone," yelled Rachael.

Frieda didn't understand why Rachael was treating her like that, but she quickly left her yard and started home. On the way, she ran into Caring Carl. "Hi, Frieda," said Carl. "What are you up to?"

"Well, I have been trying to find someone to play with, and I finally saw Rachael sitting on her steps. I asked her if she wanted to play, and she just yelled at me and told me she didn't want to be with me. I can't figure it out because the last time we played together, I thought we had a good time. She said she hadn't, so I don't know what is going on."

"Well, Frieda, Rachael is mean to me a lot. I didn't understand it either, because I try to be nice to her. But I know that I don't want to waste my time playing with her if she is mean and rude. Why don't we see if we can find something to do together?" said Carl.

"That sounds like a good idea. Maybe Likeable Lilly is home by now and would like to play with us, too," said Frieda. So Carl and Frieda ran down the street and rang Lilly's doorbell. Her mother answered the door and said that Lilly was in the back yard playing on the swings. As soon as Carl and Frieda walked into the yard, Lilly waved at them and invited them to swing. After they had done that for a while, Frieda asked Carl and Lilly if they wanted to go over to her house and play in her playhouse. They all thought that was a good idea, and off they went.

When they got to Frieda's house, she asked them if they would like a snack. While they were eating their snacks, they talked about what they wanted to do in the playhouse.

"I think it would be fun to play house," said Lilly.

"Well, that would be OK, but I'd sort of like to play hospital," said Carl.

"What if we played house for a while and then played hospital?" suggested Frieda. "Then you could both do what you wanted to."

"But what do *you* want to do, Frieda?" asked Carl. "It's not fair to just play what we want. After all, it is your playhouse."

"That's OK," said Frieda. "I like playing both of those things, and I'm just glad that you're here and we are all being nice to each other. I sure don't like to play with kids who are mean like Rachael can be."

"I agree," said Lilly. "It's a lot better to play with kids who can share and cooperate and be nice to each other. I'm glad you two are like that. Now . . . let's start playing!"

Discussion

CONTENT QUESTIONS

1. What was different about the way Caring Carl treated Friendly Frieda and the way Rude Rachael treated Friendly Frieda? Whose behavior did you think was better, and why?

2. What were some of the positive friendship behaviors that Friendly Frieda, Caring Carl, and Likeable Lilly practiced?

3. What were some of the negative friendship behaviors that Rude Rachael demonstrated?

4. Do you think Frieda tried to be a good friend to Rachael? If so, what did she do that demonstrated positive friendship behaviors?

PERSONALIZATION QUESTIONS

1. Have you ever known someone who treated you the way Rude Rachael treated Friendly Frieda? If so, how did you feel about being treated like that?

2. Do you act more like Rude Rachael or Friendly Frieda toward your friends? Which way do you think is better?

3. If someone treats you the way Rachael treated Frieda, does it mean that no one likes you? Does it mean you can't have friends?

4. Did you learn anything from this lesson that will help you be a better friend?

Follow-up Activity

Invite children to work in small groups and make up skits that demonstrate positive friendship behaviors.

Do I Have a Choice?

Developmental Perspective

At this stage of development, children are beginning to think in a more logical manner when something is presented in a concrete form. However, because they need to make choices about many things that are more abstract, helping them learn to make choices and differentiate between good, bad, and "so-so" choices is an important part of their cognitive development.

Objectives

▷ To learn that everyone makes choices based on different reasons

▷ To differentiate between good, bad, and "so-so" choices

Materials

▷ Chalkboard

▷ An empty suitcase

▷ A paper bag containing the following items: an umbrella, a night light, a book, a stuffed animal, some animal crackers, a jacket, a pair of pajamas, and a toy car

▷ Three hula hoops

▷ One tagboard sign per hoop, labeled as follows: *good choice, bad choice,* and *so-so choice*

▷ Paper and crayons for each child (for the Follow-up Activity)

Procedure

1. Introduce the lesson by bringing out the suitcase and asking children to pretend they are going on an overnight trip. Bring out the bag of items and take them out of the bag, one by one. Tell the children they need to help you choose *five* things to take on this short trip. As you pick up each item, ask them to raise a hand if this is one of the items they would want or need to take. Write the names of the items on the chalkboard and record the number of children who respond affirmatively to each.

2. After all items have been introduced, look at which items were selected most frequently and ask children if everyone chose the same items and how they made their selections. Emphasize that everyone had a choice of which five things to select, but they probably selected them for different reasons. Help them identify various reasons for their selections: preferences (some may like animal crackers, others may not), what they think they might need (some may need a night light or a stuffed animal to help them get to sleep and others don't), or what they like to do (read or play with a toy).

3. Next place the three hula hoops in the center of the room and put one of the tagboard signs beside each hoop. Divide the children into groups of five. Explain that you will be reading a choice that they should pretend they have made. After you read the choice, the first five children will decide if this would be a *good choice,* a *bad choice,* or a *so-so choice* and take a position in the hula hoop that represents their opinion. Read the next two choices and follow the same procedure with the same five children. Then take the second group of five children, read three choices, and have these children take positions. Do the same with the third group of children, and so on. (Group size and number of choices may vary depending on the size of the total group.) As children make each choice, write the choice on the chalkboard. Record the number of children in each hoop for each choice.

GOOD, BAD, AND SO-SO CHOICES

- ▶ Choosing to brush your teeth after every meal
- ▶ Choosing to study your spelling words for the test
- ▶ Choosing to eat a candy bar just before dinner
- ▶ Choosing to call someone a bad name
- ▶ Choosing to go outside in cold weather without a jacket
- ▶ Choosing to tease your little brother
- ▶ Choosing to share a toy with a friend
- ▶ Choosing to stay up past your bedtime
- ▶ Choosing to make a card for your grandfather, who is sick
- ▶ Choosing to push someone off the teeter-totter
- ▶ Choosing to run down the hall at school
- ▶ Choosing to say thank-you when your mother tells you how nice you look
- ▶ Choosing to comb and brush your hair before school pictures
- ▶ Choosing to play in the sandbox with your school clothes on
- ▶ Choosing to drink a soda pop instead of milk for supper

4. Process the activity by discussing the Content and Personalization Questions.

Discussion

CONTENT QUESTIONS

1. Does everyone have choices about lots of different things?
2. In the hula hoop activity, how did you decide if the choice was a good one, a bad one, or a so-so one?
3. In this activity, did everyone judge the choices in the same way? For example, did everyone think it was a bad choice to eat a candy bar before dinner? (Select an example based on the actual differences in the game.)

PERSONALIZATION QUESTIONS

1. What are some examples of choices you make each day that weren't identified in this activity?

2. Do you think that most of the choices you make are good ones? Bad ones? So-so ones? How do you know? What do other people think about your choices?

3. What did you learn from this lesson about choices?

Follow-up Activity

Ask children to divide a sheet of paper in half and draw a picture of a good choice and a bad choice. Post these in the room and structure time for children to share their pictures and talk about what they could have done to avoid making the bad choices.

What's the Consequence?

Developmental Perspective

Although children are gradually developing the ability to understand logical operations, reversibility, and reciprocity, they are not always able to apply these concepts in a consistent manner in their day-to-day activities. Because they are spending more time at school and away from home, teaching them how to think logically and anticipate consequences is important.

Objectives

▷ To learn to identify consequences of behavior

▷ To learn to distinguish between positive and negative consequences

Materials

▷ Four balloons (one filled with water)

▷ A newsprint version of the What's the Consequence? Chart (Handout 6; for the Follow-up Activity)

Procedure

1. Introduce the lesson by asking children to predict what will happen in each of the four following balloon experiments. After they have done so, perform the experiments to confirm or disconfirm their predictions.

   ▶ Experiment 1: What if I blow this balloon up, don't tie the end, and let it go?

   ▶ Experiment 2: What if I blow this balloon up, tie the end, and let it go?

   ▶ Experiment 3: What if I bop this blown-up balloon hard with my hand on its right side? Left? Bottom? Top?

   ▶ Experiment 4: What if I take this balloon filled with water, tie the end, and throw it on the ground?

2. Ask what each of the balloon demonstrations proves. Discuss the fact that in each instance there was a *consequence* of the action taken, and that many of them were able to successfully predict the consequence.

3. Read the following, asking children to predict a consequence for each:

   ▶ You look at your sister and stick your tongue out.

   ▶ You tattle to the teacher.

   ▶ You are friendly to other children.

   ▶ You help others when they need help.

   ▶ You cry when you don't get your way.

> ► You constantly ask questions even if you know the answer or could figure it out.

> ► You pout when you are angry.

> ► You eat junk food when you aren't supposed to.

> ► You stay up past your bedtime every night.

> ► You offer to take turns on the merry-go-round.

4. Next read the following story aloud to the children. Stop at the pauses identified in the story to elicit consequences.

WHAT'S THE CONSEQUENCE?

Elena had just gotten a new blue bicycle for her birthday, and she was so anxious to ride it! She begged her stepmother to let her ride over to the park, but her stepmother told her that since they were going to eat soon, Elena wouldn't have enough time to go to the park but she could ride around the block if she promised not to stop off at anyone's house. "I promise," said Elena, who was really excited to go.

So off she went on her new blue bike. It felt so good to ride! As soon as she rounded the first corner she saw Pedro and José playing catch in their front yard. "Hey, guys," shouted Elena. "Look what my dad and stepmom gave me for my birthday!" "Wow, it looks neat. Stop so we can see it," said Pedro. So Elena stopped. *(Elicit consequences.)*

After Pedro and José had admired her new bike, Elena said that she had to keep going because it was almost time for dinner. She pedaled away, and before she got to the next corner, she saw her best friend, Megan, chasing a puppy around the yard. Elena quickly put on her brakes and got off her bike. "Oh, what an adorable puppy. Is it yours?" asked Elena. "Yes, we just picked her up this afternoon," said Megan. "Do you want to hold her?" Elena couldn't resist, so she picked up the puppy and petted her until the puppy fell asleep. *(Elicit consequences.)*

Suddenly, Elena remembered that she was supposed to go straight home, so she jumped on her bike and rode away. Now she was getting worried because she had stopped at Pedro and José's and at Megan's, so she pedaled faster and faster. As the next corner came up, she was going at a pretty fast pace. *(Elicit consequences.)*

Suddenly, there was a little boy in a wagon ahead of her. Elena tried rounding the corner, but she had to swerve to avoid colliding with the boy, and she fell off her bike. *(Elicit consequences.)*

Elena picked herself up. She had a skinned knee, and her elbow was bleeding a little. She slowly got back on her bike and headed home. When she got to her driveway, her dad was standing in front of the garage. *(Elicit consequences.)*

Elena put her bike away, went inside and washed up, and sat down to supper. Her dad and stepmom talked to her about what had happened and told her that since she had disobeyed, she wouldn't be able to ride her bike for two days. Elena was so angry that she jumped up from the table and knocked over her glass of milk. *(Elicit consequences.)*

Elena got sent to her room and was told to think about her choices. Do you think she made good ones? Were there some bad consequences as a result of her choices? *(Discuss.)*

5. Process the activity by discussing the Content and Personalization Questions.

Discussion

CONTENT QUESTIONS

1. What is a consequence? Can consequences be both good and bad?
2. Can you change a consequence? If so, how?
3. Can you stop a consequence from occurring? If so, how?
4. Why is it important to think about consequences before you do something?

PERSONALIZATION QUESTIONS

1. Can you think of a choice you have made that had a good consequence? (Invite sharing of examples.)
2. Can you think of a choice you have made that had a bad consequence? (Invite sharing of examples.)
3. If you have had more bad than good consequences, is there anything you can do to change this? If so, what do you need to do?

Follow-up Activity

Post the newsprint version of the What's the Consequence? Chart (Handout 6) in the room. At a designated time each day for a week, ask children to identify behaviors and consequences for that day. Allow time for discussion about how to change behaviors if the consequences were negative.

What's the Consequence?

CHART

	Behaviors	Consequences
Monday		
Tuesday		
Wednesday		
Thursday		
Friday		

Solutions, Solutions

Developmental Perspective

Because children this age are in the concrete-thinking stage, it is often difficult for them to identify a variety of alternatives. This can significantly limit their ability to problem solve, which in turn affects them in many different aspects of their lives.

Objectives

▷ To recognize that many problems have multiple solutions

▷ To develop skills in identifying multiple solutions to typical problems

Materials

▷ Chalkboard

▷ Paper and pencil for each child

▷ Several magnifying glasses

▷ Four large tagboard shapes: circle, square, triangle, and rectangle

Procedure

1. Introduce this lesson by informing children that they will be going on a scavenger hunt (outside if possible) for shapes. Divide children into four groups. Hold up the circle shape and designate one group to be circles. Do the same for the other three shapes. Then explain that the groups are to look around and find as many examples as possible of their specific shape in a 15-minute time period. (They will not actually collect those that are too large or awkward to move.) Their examples can be larger or smaller than the shapes used for the demonstration, and they may want to use a magnifying glass to help them locate the smaller examples.

2. After the time is up, bring children together to share what they discovered. Conduct the sharing and discussion as follows:

   ▶ Ask all children who were hunting for *circles* to stand. Ask several children to share their examples and list these on the chalkboard under a circle shape.

   ▶ Ask all children who were hunting for *squares* to stand. Ask several children to share their examples and list these on the chalkboard under a square shape.

   ▶ Ask children who were hunting for *triangles* to stand. Ask several children to share their examples and list these on the chalkboard under a triangle shape.

> ▶ Ask children who were hunting for *rectangles* to stand. Ask several children to share their examples and list these on the chalkboard under a rectangle shape.

3. Ask children if there was more than one solution or answer for each shape. Emphasize the fact that most problems have more than one solution, then ask children to elaborate on the concept by sharing some examples of problems that have more than one solution.

4. Read the following story aloud to the children. When you have finished reading, write each of the italicized problems on the chalkboard. Engage children in brainstorming as many solutions as possible for each of the identified items.

> Sally needed solutions. Every morning her mom or her dad yelled up the stairs to tell her to wake up, but Sally usually fell back to sleep again. She didn't know what to do that would help her *wake up on time*. When she finally did get up, she usually had problems deciding what to wear. She would stand in front of her closet for a long time trying to figure out *what to put on*. After she finally got dressed, she sat at the breakfast table for a long time. She had lots of choices, but she didn't know how to decide *what to eat*. Finally, she was almost ready for school, but she needed to decide *what to take for show-and-tell*.

5. Process the activity by asking the Content and Personalization Questions.

Discussion

CONTENT QUESTIONS

1. Is it possible for a problem to have more than one solution?
2. Why is it best to try and find as many solutions as possible?
3. How can you figure out different solutions to problems?

PERSONALIZATION QUESTIONS

1. Do you have a problem that you can't think of solutions for? Did any of the ideas that were shared in this lesson give you ideas of what to do?
2. If you have a problem and can't think of solutions, what should you do? Are there others who can help you with solutions?

Follow-up Activity

At the end of each day for a week, ask one or two children to share a problem they would like solutions for. Engage other children in helping generate multiple solutions.

What Should I Do?

Developmental Perspective

During this period, children gradually develop the ability to think more logically. They are not as egocentric, nor do they hold such a magical view of the world as they did when preschoolers. Despite the fact that they are better able to gather and organize information, they encounter more challenges as they begin to venture out more and explore their environment. Knowing what to do can be a dilemma.

Objective

▷ To develop problem-solving skills

Materials

▷ Chalkboard
▷ Three signs made out of tagboard or construction paper, labeled as follows: *choices, consequences,* and *solution*

Procedure

1. Initiate discussion by asking children to raise a hand if they have ever had trouble deciding what to do about something. Invite sharing of examples.

2. Next review the concepts from Activities 2 and 3 regarding consequences and multiple solutions. Explain that children will need to use this information in this lesson.

3. Divide children into groups of three. Explain that you will be reading some problem situations. After you have read a problem, you will hold up a sign and each group will discuss that aspect of the problem. First they will be discussing the different *choices* the child in the scenario has. Then they will be discussing the *consequences* for these choices, and finally they will be selecting what they consider to be the best *solution* to the problem.

4. Read the first of the following scenarios. Hold up the first sign *(choices)* and allow several minutes for each group to discuss. Ask each group to share the choices they identified. List these on the chalkboard. Then hold up the second sign *(consequences)* and have groups identify consequences. List these on the chalkboard next to their respective choices. Then invite each group to look at all the choices and consequences and to select what they consider to be the best solution. Have each group share their solution and discuss why they selected this option.

WHAT SHOULD I DO? SCENARIOS

> ▶ You can only invite five kids to your birthday party, and there are eight that you play with regularly. What should you do?
>
> ▶ You are at an amusement park with your older cousin. She wants to ride the roller coaster, but you are afraid to go. You don't want your cousin to think you are a scaredy cat. What should you do?
>
> ▶ Your dad and mom are yelling and arguing. You are afraid your dad will hit your mom. What should you do?
>
> ▶ You have been invited to spend the night with a friend, but you aren't sure you want to go because sometimes you get scared in the night. What should you do?
>
> ▶ Your friend tells you a secret that you promised not to tell, but you think maybe you should because she did something bad. What should you do?
>
> ▶ You are supposed to be in bed at 8:30, but your parents are gone and you think you can talk the baby-sitter into letting you stay up to watch one of your favorite television shows. Your parents said you had to go to bed early since you are going on a trip tomorrow. What should you do?

5. Follow this same procedure for the other scenarios, then discuss the Content and Personalization Questions.

Discussion

CONTENT QUESTIONS

1. Which was hardest for your group to identify: choices, consequences, or the best solution?
2. Do you think it would be good to solve a problem without looking at all the choices and consequences? What might happen if you didn't?
3. Do you think all problems have good solutions? Can you think of some that might not?

PERSONALIZATION QUESTIONS

1. When you try to solve a problem, do you look at all the choices and consequences?
2. How do you usually feel about the solutions you come up with?
3. What is the most difficult problem you have ever had to solve? How did you feel about the solution?
4. When you have difficult problems to solve, do you ask others for help?
5. What did you learn from this lesson that can help you in your problem-solving process?

Follow-up Activity

Apply this process to problems that come up in the classroom, emphasizing the three-step procedure of choices, consequences, and solution.

the **PASSPORT** PROGRAM

GRADE 2

Self-Development
ACTIVITY
1   Dial "M" for "Me"
2   It's Me!
3   I Count
4   Hand It to Me

Emotional Development
ACTIVITY
1   New Experiences
2   I Feel Dumb
3   Mad Management
4   A Lot or a Little?

Social Development
ACTIVITY
1   All Kinds of Families
2   Friendship Facts
3   Friends Come in All Shapes and Sizes
4   Circles of Friendship

Cognitive Development
ACTIVITY
1   What's the Problem?
2   Is That a Fact?
3   Decisions, Decisions, Decisions
4   Other Options

Dial "M" for "Me"

Developmental Perspective

During middle childhood, various aspects of children's personalities are developing. At this age, children are more aware of their own skill development, and they make judgments about their appearance, abilities, and other attributes. It is important to help them expand their awareness of themselves in a variety of different areas and learn to accept themselves.

Objectives

▷ To develop awareness of abilities and attributes

▷ To learn to accept oneself with these abilities and attributes

Materials

▷ Thirteen 5 × 8–inch index cards with a string attached to each to form necklaces. The cards should be labeled as follows (one item per card):

    A: An activity you do well

    B: Something you are proud of concerning your behavior

    C: Something you can do well in school

    D: Something you don't do very well

    E: Something you are excited about doing or learning

    F: Something that frightens you

    G: One way in which you have grown since last year

    H: Something you are happy about

    I: One way you use your imagination

    J: Something you just wish you could do better

    K: A way in which you have been kind to someone else

    L: Something you like about the way you treat others

    M: Something you like about yourself

▷ A soda bottle

▷ Additional index cards (for the Follow-up Activity)

Procedure

1. Ask for 13 volunteers. Give each volunteer one of the alphabet necklaces. Seat these children in a circle. If there are more players, they may also sit in the circle. If there are fewer, each volunteer can wear more than one card.

2. Select a child to be "It." This child spins the bottle. When it lands, the child who is "It" looks at the child seated in the spot where the bottle points, reads the card that child is wearing, and responds. (If the bottle points toward a person without a necklace, the child spins again.) Continue with a second child who is "It" and proceed with the game until all children have had at least one turn to spin.

3. To process the activity, ask the Content and Personalization Questions.

Discussion

CONTENT QUESTIONS

1. Was it difficult for you to think of what to say when it was your turn to spin?

2. What did you learn about someone else while you were playing this game?

3. What did you learn about yourself while you were playing this game?

PERSONALIZATION QUESTIONS

1. What do you like best about your abilities and attributes?

2. Suppose there are some things you wish you could do better or would like to change about yourself. Does that mean you should think of yourself as awful or terrible, or does it mean that you should accept yourself as a kid with both positive or negative points?

Follow-up Activity

Make letters for the rest of the alphabet and play the game again.

It's Me!

Developmental Perspective

At this stage of development, children are likely to give you a list of concrete, observable characteristics if you ask them to describe how they see themselves. As they get older, they will also be able to refer to psychological traits. Their awareness of themselves is expanding during this period, and because their thinking is very concrete they are likely to evaluate themselves as either good or bad, competent or incompetent. In order for them to develop a positive yet realistic self-concept, it is important to help them accept themselves for both their strengths and limitations.

Objectives

▷ To recognize that strengths and limitations are part of one's self-definition

▷ To learn not to put oneself down because of limitations

Materials

▷ Two butcher paper cutouts of a T-shirt for each child (one for the front and one for the back). These will be stapled together at the shoulders once children have completed the activity.

▷ Crayons and/or a pencil for each child

Procedure

1. Distribute the materials to each child and indicate that children are going to be making an "It's Me" T-shirt.

2. Ask children to think about ways they would describe themselves: things they like to do, things they do well, things they are learning to do, and things they can't do too well. Ask them to draw pictures or write words on their paper T-shirts to illustrate these points.

3. When they are finished, staple the two pieces of each shirt together at the shoulders so that the drawings are on the outside. Have children put their names somewhere on the shirts.

4. Next, as in a fashion show, invite each child to come to the front of the room, slowly turn around, and then walk through the room so others may observe what he or she has drawn.

5. Process the activity by asking the Content and Personalization Questions.

Discussion

CONTENT QUESTIONS

1. What is something you like to do?
2. What is something you do well?
3. What is something you don't do too well?
4. What is something you are learning to do?

PERSONALIZATION QUESTIONS

1. How do you feel about the things you put on your T-shirt? Do you like being you?
2. What does it say about you if there are some things you don't do too well? Does this mean you are a "no-good" kid? Do you suppose all people have some things they can't do as well as other things?

Follow-up Activity

Display the T-shirts and encourage children to consider how others have identified themselves.

I Count

Developmental Perspective

Middle childhood is an important formative period with regard to self-concept. Parents have great influence over their children's view of themselves. Unfortunately, many children grow up in dysfunctional families where parents don't validate their children. It is therefore important to help children see that they are important or special to many people in their lives, including themselves.

Objectives

▷ To identify ways each person is important to others

▷ To learn to accept oneself regardless of others' views

Materials

▷ A copy of the I Count–Chart (Handout 1) and a pencil for each child

▷ The following master list on poster paper or the chalkboard:

    A: Is a good helper

    B: Tries hard to learn things

    C: Gets along well with brothers and/or sisters

    D: Is a good listener

    E: Shares toys, books, or games with other children

    F: Takes turns when playing

    G: Says nice things about other people

    H: Uses good manners (says "please" and "thank-you")

    I: Does things when asked to do so (such as pick up toys, go to bed)

    J: Tells the truth

    K: Is fun to play with

Procedure

1. Introduce the lesson by explaining that there are many different people in children's lives who think they are important or special, and that the purpose of this lesson is to help them identify how they are important to others.

2. Give each child an I Count–Chart (Handout 1). Read the categories to familiarize children with what they will be marking on the chart.

3. Explain that you will read the first item: "Is a good helper" (alphabet letter *A*). Children are to think about who on that chart would think they are a good helper and put an *X* beside each of these people's names under the alphabet letter *A* (there may be more than one). Continue with the second item (alphabet letter *B*). Proceed until all items have been read and children have completed their charts.

4. To process the activity, ask the Content and Personalization Questions.

Discussion

CONTENT QUESTIONS

1. Was it hard for you to identify people who might think you were good in these areas? Were some areas more difficult than others to do? (Invite sharing.)

2. Which item did you have the most *X*'s for (count down the page under each alphabet letter)? Which item did you have the least *X*'s for?

PERSONALIZATION QUESTIONS

1. Do you now think you are more important to lots of people than you thought you were before doing this activity?

2. Do you think it is possible to be special or important in all areas to everyone?

3. Even if someone else thinks you are not important or special, does that mean that you are not OK? What does it mean?

4. What did you learn about yourself from this lesson?

Follow-up Activity

Invite children to ask parents, stepparents, grandparents, or siblings to tell children how they are special or important.

I Count

CHART

Name: _____ Date: _____

	A	B	C	D	E	F	G	H	I	J	K
Mom											
Dad											
Stepmom											
Stepdad											
Brother											
Sister											
Grandma											
Grandpa											
Uncle											
Aunt											
Teacher											
Baby-sitter											
Friend											

Hand It to Me

Developmental Perspective

As children begin to compare their skills and achievements to those of others, they may become self-critical or feel inferior. As they strive to achieve new skills, they are subject not only to their own self-evaluation, but to feedback from peers as well. Because a positive yet realistic self-concept is such an important cornerstone of development, it is important to help children identify positive things they can remember about themselves when they are feeling vulnerable.

Objectives

▷ To identify individual strengths
▷ To learn a strategy to help remember good things about oneself

Materials

▷ A sheet of drawing paper, pencil, and crayons for each child
▷ Paper and crayons (for the Follow-up Activity)

Procedure

1. Begin this lesson by distributing paper, pencils, and crayons and having children trace around both their hands.
2. Next talk with them about how it is sometimes easy for them to feel bad because they think they can't do some things as well as their classmates or their friends, or because classmates, friends, or even adults may put them down by saying they aren't very good at something. Invite children to share about times they might have felt this way.
3. Explain that since they can't control what other people say to them, it is important to have some things they can do to help themselves when they feel bad about their abilities, their performance, or their behavior.
4. Ask children to hold out one of their hands, palm up. Have them think of five things they do well, emphasizing that no one does everything perfectly. Thus, a child might identify "Is a good runner," even though he or she could be faster and maybe will be when older. After children have thought of five things, they should write one item on each finger of one of their hand outlines. Repeat the procedure and have them do the same for the other hand.
5. Ask children to hold out their hands, palms up. Show children that the next time someone says something that makes them feel bad about themselves, they can think about what they wrote on their hand outlines and remember all the good things about themselves.
6. Process the activity by asking the Content and Personalization Questions.

Discussion

CONTENT QUESTIONS

1. Was it easy for you to think of things you do well?

2. If it wasn't easy, why do you think it wasn't?

3. Why do you think it is important to remember the things you do well?

4. Even if someone says something about you that you don't like, does that mean that you are no good? If the person says, for example, that you are dumb in math, does it mean you are a dumb kid, that you are no good, or that you are even necessarily dumb in math?

PERSONALIZATION QUESTIONS

1. What can you do the next time someone says something about you that makes you feel bad about yourself?

2. What did you learn from this lesson?

Follow-up Activity

Invite children to write a story, draw a picture, or make up a song about a time they performed well in one of the areas they listed on their hand outlines.

New Experiences

Developmental Perspective

There are lots of "firsts" during this period of development: going to school all day and having more rigorous academic work, joining groups, taking lessons, participating in team sports, or staying overnight at a friend's house. Depending on the child, there can be varying degrees of anxiety associated with peer interaction, competition, and mastery of skills. Children need to learn how to take risks and at the same time express and deal with feelings of anxiety or uncertainty associated with these experiences. Concrete cognition makes it difficult for children to look at all aspects of a situation; however, in order to deal effectively with apprehension it is important that they learn to do so.

Objectives

▷ To express feelings about new experiences

▷ To learn coping skills for dealing with new experiences

Materials

▷ Four empty cereal boxes, each containing a strip of paper with one of the following situations written on it:

Staying overnight at a friend's house for the first time

Playing in your first Little League game or piano recital

Taking your first test

Joining a new group where you don't know many kids or the leader

▷ Twenty blank strips of paper and a pencil

▷ Paper and crayons for each child (for the Follow-up Activity)

Procedure

1. Introduce the activity by discussing the experience of losing a tooth. After some discussion, explain that as children get older they will have lots of new experiences, some of which may be similar to losing a tooth. Sometimes they will be excited about these new experiences, but sometimes they may be a little afraid because they don't know what these experiences will be like.

2. Bring out the first box and open it, taking out the strip of paper and reading the situation. Have children raise their hands if they have experienced this situation.

3. Next discuss how children felt when they were in this situation for the first time. Then take a few of the blank strips of paper and invite children to share what they were thinking or might think about that experience. (Examples for staying overnight might be as follows: "What if I get scared?" "What if I have to go to the bathroom and don't remember where it is?" "What if I don't like the food they have?" "What if I miss my mom or dad?") Write these on the blank strips as children share.

4. Then ask children who have experienced the situation if they have suggestions for dealing with any bad feelings they might have had. After they have shared ideas, teach children coping self-statements to help in the future. Coping self-statements for fears about staying overnight might include "If I get really scared, I can always tell my friend's parent, and she could help me"; "If I don't remember where the bathroom is, I can just ask"; "If I don't like the food, I can eat just a little bit or just leave it on my plate"; and "If I miss my mom or dad, I could call. I won't be gone that long anyway."

5. Use the same procedure for the other boxes. Have children identify coping self-statements for these situations as well, then discuss the Content and Personalization Questions.

Discussion

CONTENT QUESTIONS

1. What are some more examples of things you can say to yourself if you are afraid of the new experiences discussed today?

2. Did you learn anything from other children about how to help yourself handle new situations in a positive way?

PERSONALIZATION QUESTIONS

1. What are some examples of new situations you have felt scared or uncertain about?

2. What did you do in these new situations to help yourself feel less scared or uncertain?

3. Once you have been in a new situation, have you been as scared the second time? If not, what does that say to you about new experiences?

Follow-up Activity

Ask children to divide a sheet of paper in half. On one side of the paper they are to draw a picture of a situation they have had some negative feelings about. On the other side they are to write at least three coping self-statements they used or could use to help them deal with this type of situation.

I Feel Dumb

Developmental Perspective

Children begin to experience the need for mastery when they are in the primary grades. Generally, this is their initial encounter with evaluation in the form of stars, stickers, or letter grades. They are learning to read, write, and do math, among many other things. With these new opportunities may come apprehension about their ability to master tasks. In addition, children at this age are concrete thinkers, and they readily make assumptions about their abilities or others' expectations for their performance. Because the assumptions are often based on limited information (a result of their inability to see a range of alternatives) anxiety may arise.

Objectives

▷ To learn ways to deal with anxiety about performance in school-related tasks

▷ To learn that poor performance does not necessarily make someone a "bad kid"

Materials

▷ One shoe box, construction paper, crayons, scissors, and glue for each child (for the Follow-up Activity)

Procedure

1. Recruit three volunteers who are wearing shoes with ties to be "students" and one volunteer to be "teacher."

2. Invite the student volunteers to sit in the front and the teacher volunteer to stand in front of them. The teacher volunteer asks the students to untie and then retie their shoes. Before they do this, instruct the teacher volunteer in private to be mean and critical to one volunteer, praise another and say what a good job that person is doing, and not pay any attention to the third one.

3. Following the role-play, ask the student volunteers how they felt about how the teacher volunteer treated them. Did they think the way they were treated had anything to do with the way in which they tied their shoes? Did the student whom the teacher praised feel smarter than the other two? Did the ones who were ignored and criticized feel not as capable as the other student? Point out that since all three knew how to tie their shoes, the way the teacher treated them didn't mean they weren't capable of performing the task. Ask, "Just because the teacher treated only one of them nicely, does that mean the other two are bad kids?" Reinforce the idea that how someone else treats them doesn't necessarily reflect on their performance, and that even if they do perform poorly, it doesn't mean they are bad kids.

4. Read the following story aloud to the children, then discuss the Content and Personalization Questions.

I FEEL DUMB

It was August, just a few weeks before school was going to start. Nicole, who was going into second grade, didn't even want to think about it. Her first-grade teacher had been mean, and Nicole thought that the teacher didn't like her because sometimes Nicole made mistakes on her reading assignments. She had seen Mrs. Winters, her first-grade teacher, talking to Mr. Rivera, the second-grade teacher. She figured that Mrs. Winters had told him all about the mistakes Nicole made, so she thought that Mr. Rivera probably wouldn't like her either.

One night Nicole couldn't get to sleep for a long time because she was thinking about this problem. All at once, she had an idea. Maybe she could go and live with her dad and her stepmother. That way she wouldn't have to go to school at West Elementary, and she wouldn't have to have a teacher who didn't like her. That idea sounded good for a while, but then she thought about the fact that maybe another teacher in a different school wouldn't like her either because sometimes she made mistakes. So once again she had no solution.

That weekend she went to visit her dad. When he asked her if she was excited about starting second grade, she started to cry. Finally, she was able to tell her dad about how mean Mrs. Winters had been, and how she was afraid that if she made mistakes, her second-grade teacher would be mean and wouldn't like her. Her dad just listened, and then he got up and walked over to the refrigerator. He came back to the table with several different kinds of fruit and a basket. He put these on the table and asked Nicole to examine each piece of fruit and put it in the basket. When she was finished, he asked her if all the fruit in the basket was perfect: Were there some oranges that had brown spots on them? Were there some grapes that were shriveled up? Were there some bright red, shiny apples? When Nicole agreed that some of the fruit was not perfect, her dad explained to her that kids are like fruit: Sometimes they do perfect work, sometimes they do almost perfect work, and sometimes they don't do very well. But even if kids do poorly, it doesn't mean that they are bad kids, just like the fruit in the basket isn't all bad. He explained to her that teachers expect kids to make some mistakes because that's how kids learn; it doesn't mean that the teacher doesn't like them.

After hearing this, Nicole felt a little better. She decided that she would do her best, but even if she didn't always do well, it wouldn't mean that the teacher didn't like her. She felt better for several days, but every once in a while the worries would start coming back. She didn't always feel like talking about them, so she decided to make a

"Worry Box." She found a shoe box and covered it with paper. She cut a hole in the top. Whenever she started to worry about things such as her teacher's not liking her, she wrote down the worry and put it in the box. Then at the end of the week she checked to see what was in her box. If she was still worried about those things, she talked them over with her mom or her dad, and this made her feel better. She especially remembered what her mother had once told her—that just because Mrs. Winters had sometimes been mean doesn't mean Mr. Rivera would be. That made sense to Nicole, so she kept telling herself that every time she started to worry.

By the end of the summer, Nicole even felt a little excited about going to school. She realized that second grade could be different than first, and she now knew that her teacher would like her even if she sometimes made mistakes.

Discussion

CONTENT QUESTIONS

1. Why was Nicole feeling so bad about second grade?
2. What did her dad do with her to help her see that she couldn't be perfect all the time?
3. What did her dad say to her to help her see that teachers still liked kids even if they didn't always get everything right?
4. Why did Nicole start to feel better about going to second grade?

PERSONALIZATION QUESTIONS

1. Have you ever felt the same way Nicole did?
2. If you have felt like that, what did you do to help yourself feel better about the situation?
3. What did you learn from Nicole's story that you can use to help you if you ever have problems like this?

Follow-up Activity

Have each child make a "Worry Box" to use as needed.

Mad Management

Developmental Perspective

Feeling angry is not uncommon at this age, but children need to learn appropriate ways to manage their angry feelings so they don't behave inappropriately and create more problems for themselves.

Objective

▷ To learn appropriate ways to manage mad feelings

Materials

▷ Puppets or materials to make paper bag or sock puppets
(for the Follow-up Activity)

Procedure

1. Ask children to raise their hands if they have ever experienced mad feelings. Invite a few children to share examples of situations.

2. Read the following story aloud, then discuss the Content and Personalization Questions.

MOE THE MAD MOOSE

It was a sunny fall day in the north woods. Moe was looking forward to wandering around and just having a lazy day. He thought he would try to find his friend Molly Moose and maybe they could play with little Mikey Moose. So Moe told Mama Moose he would be back later, and off he went.

Now most of the other moose liked Moe because he was easy to get along with. He didn't get mad when someone didn't want to play with him; he just found someone else who wanted to play. He didn't get mad if the others didn't want to play the games he wanted to play; he just went along with their ideas or found someone else who was interested in what he wanted to play. And Moe didn't even get mad if another moose took over his territory; he just got up and moved on because it wasn't a big deal to him.

But on this nice sunny fall day in the north woods, Moe's friends were shocked because Moe got very mad. Moe got so mad that his father, who was taking a walk through the woods and was quite far away, heard him roar. Not only did his father hear him, but so did his cousin, and he lived clear across the lake. Moe was so mad he just kept on roaring and roaring. Now, what do you think made Moe so mad? *(Elicit ideas from the children.)*

Well, the reason Moe was so mad was that when he and Molly and Mikey were together, three very big moose with big antlers came over to the field where they were playing and started poking at little Mikey Moose with their antlers. Mikey was scared, and Molly and Moe were afraid these bigger moose would hurt little Mikey. They didn't think it was fair for the big ones to pick on a little one, and that was why Moe was so mad.

Now Moe had seen his brother Milton Moose when Milton got mad. He knew that Milton had once been so mad that he had rammed another moose into a tree. But when their father found out about that, Milton got in big trouble. Papa Moose told Milton that no matter how mad you were, you shouldn't hurt another moose. Moe also knew that another time when Milton was mad he just ran away from home. Once again Papa Moose scolded Milton and told him that he needed to find better ways to manage his mad feelings. So what do you think Moe did to manage his mad feelings? *(Elicit ideas from the children.)*

Well, first of all, you know that he roared and roared. That helped him a little, and it didn't really hurt anyone else. But after he roared, he also ran around the woods to help him get rid of some of the mad feelings. But he also did something else. He went home and wrote a letter telling the big moose that he didn't want them to hurt his friend. He didn't call them names in the letter or say anything bad about them because he thought that would make the big moose angry. After he finished writing the letter, he showed it to Mama Moose. She liked what he had written and agreed that it was a good idea to let the other moose know how he felt about what they did. She told him that sometimes other moose do things that he might not think are right, but he usually can't change how they act. She told him that she was proud of the way he was handling his feelings because when something similar happened to Milton, Milton had just made things worse by starting a fight with the moose who had picked on his friend. Mama Moose encouraged Moe to keep thinking about other good ways to handle his feelings so he would have some choices if he ever got mad again.

Discussion

CONTENT QUESTIONS

1. What three things did Moe do to help him manage his mad feelings?

2. What else do you think Moe could have done in this situation?

3. Did you agree with Mama and Papa Moose that the way Milton handled his mad feelings wasn't very good? Why or why not?

PERSONALIZATION QUESTIONS

1. Have you ever had mad feelings?

2. When you have been mad, what have you done to manage your feelings?

3. Did you learn anything from this story that might help you with your mad feelings? If so, what would you like to try the next time you feel mad?

Follow-up Activity

Divide children into small groups and have them develop a puppet play about good ways to handle mad feelings. Provide time for them to present their puppet plays to the rest of the group. Debrief with discussion about appropriate versus inappropriate ways to manage angry feelings.

A Lot or a Little?

Developmental Perspective

At this age, children are very concrete thinkers. Consequently, it is difficult for them to understand the concept of a continuum of feelings. As a result, they frequently assume that someone is either very mad or very happy about something, without recognizing the range of intensity of emotions. Without this understanding, misinterpretation is not uncommon. It is possible to teach children techniques to help them see a broader perspective.

Objectives

▷ To learn to differentiate the intensity of emotions

▷ To learn that everyone doesn't feel the same way about the same situation

Materials

▷ Chalkboard

▷ A ruler, a sheet of paper, and a pencil for each child

▷ Another sheet of paper per child (for the Follow-up Activity)

Procedure

1. Introduce the activity by having children use their rulers to draw a line across their papers. (Draw one on the chalkboard to serve as a model.)

2. On the model line, write the words *very happy* on one end and the words *very unhappy* on the other end. Write the other words on the line as illustrated:

| very happy | pretty happy | pretty unhappy | very unhappy |

⬅———————————————————————➡

Have children write these same words on their lines.

3. Ask children to listen carefully as you read the following situations, one at a time. After each, they are to put an X on the line to illustrate how they might feel if they were in this situation: very happy, pretty happy, pretty unhappy, very unhappy.

   ▶ Your teacher tells you that you did very well on your spelling test.
   ▶ Your sister gets to stay up later than you do.
   ▶ Your best friend didn't walk to school with you today.
   ▶ Your father yelled at you because you hadn't picked up your room.
   ▶ Your neighbor's dog chewed your new tennis shoe.
   ▶ Your big brother took you for a ride on his bike.
   ▶ Your cousin let you use her new rollerblades.

> ► You can't go out for recess because it is raining.
> ► Your class is going on a field trip to the zoo.
> ► You missed two problems on your math paper.

When you have finished reading the first situation, ask children to raise a hand if they marked this situation very happy, pretty happy, and so on. Count each response and put the total on the chalkboard beside each feeling on the continuum. Then proceed to the next situation and follow the same procedure of identifying and tallying responses.

4. After all situations have been read and recorded, process the activity by asking the Content and Personalization Questions.

Discussion

CONTENT QUESTIONS

1. Looking back at the responses, did this group have all of the marks on the *very happy* end of the line? Did this group have all of the marks on the *very unhappy* end of the line? Why do you think this group had marks at several different places on the line?

2. Was it hard for you to decide how you felt about some of these situations? If so, why do you think it was hard?

3. Do you think everyone always feels the same way about the same things? Why or why not?

PERSONALIZATION QUESTIONS

1. Think about your day today. Have you felt only very happy or very unhappy, or have you also felt pretty happy or pretty unhappy?

2. Have you ever had a disagreement with someone because that person felt differently about something than you did? (Invite sharing of examples.)

3. Based on this lesson, what do you need to remember about feelings?

Follow-up Activity

Have children take another sheet of paper and make the same continuum they did for the activity. At the end of the day, ask them to think about their afternoon and identify how they felt about different things they experienced.

All Kinds of Families

Developmental Perspective

In today's society, fewer children live in traditional family structures. It is important for them to recognize and appreciate the fact that there are many different family structures. This understanding will help children avoid feeling different or self-conscious about their own families.

Objectives

▷ To identify a wide range of family structures

▷ To identify things to appreciate about one's own family structure

Materials

▷ Chalkboard

▷ A copy of the children's story "Goldilocks and the Three Bears"

▷ Two sheets of drawing paper and two pieces of gold ribbon (large enough to paste around the drawing paper) for each child

▷ Glue, scissors, and crayons for each child

▷ A roll of masking tape

▷ Several children's books that illustrate different family structures (for the Follow-up Activity)

Procedure

1. Introduce this lesson by reading the familiar story "Goldilocks and the Three Bears." Ask children to describe the family structure represented in this story. Write the word *traditional* on the chalkboard as they describe this family structure. Ask them if they know of any other kinds of families. As children describe various family configurations, make up a suitable, age-appropriate title for each and list it on the board (for example, "single parent," "mom and dad family" or "stepfamily with kids from two families").

2. Discuss with children what makes a family a family–love, caring, sharing space and resources, and so on. List characteristics on the board as children generate them.

3. Distribute the paper and other materials. Have children draw two family portraits–the first of their own family and the second of a family very different from theirs. Have them glue the gold ribbon around the drawings to make two framed pictures.

4. Tape the pictures on the wall and have students silently walk past them as if they were viewing an art exhibit.

5. Process the activity by asking the Content and Personalization Questions.

Discussion

CONTENT QUESTIONS

1. What makes a family a family?
2. Are all families the same?
3. Can family structures change? If so, how?

PERSONALIZATION QUESTIONS

1. Which kind of family would you most like to belong to? Why?
2. What are some of the special things about your family?
3. What's something you are especially proud of concerning your family?

Follow-up Activity

Read several more stories to the children that illustrate various family structures. Examples include *Changing Families: A Guide for Kids and Grown-ups,* by David Fassler (Waterfront Books, 1988); *Good Answers to Tough Questions about Stepfamilies,* by Joy Berry (Children's Press, 1990); and *Good-bye, Daddy!* by Bridgette Weninger (North-South Books, 1995).

Friendship Facts

Developmental Perspective

As children enter second grade, friendships become increasingly important. However, many children lack skills in forming and maintaining friendships. Early and ongoing instruction in this critical area can enhance children's relationships and lead to more satisfying outcomes in their social development.

Objective

▷ To identify characteristics of friendship

Materials

▷ Four sheets of newsprint with the following categories listed, one per sheet of paper:

   A good friend is someone who . . .

   A good friend doesn't . . .

   Problems friends can have are . . .

   Friends can solve problems by . . .

▷ A dozen bottle caps, paper clips, or other sort of tokens per child

▷ A lunch-size milk carton for each child

▷ Paper and crayons for each child (for the Follow-up Activity)

Procedure

1. Introduce the lesson by asking for two volunteers to role-play making a new friend on the first day of second grade, during lunch or on the playground.

2. Analyze the role-play together by using the following questions to prompt discussion:

   ► What did the two children say to show that they were interested in becoming friends?

   ► What did the two children do to show that they wanted to be friends?

3. Next post the first sheet of newsprint and elicit a discussion about the topic: "A good friend is someone who . . ." Write the characteristics children share on the newsprint. Follow the same procedure for the other three topics.

4. Following the discussion, distribute the milk cartons and tokens. Explain that you will be reading statements about friendships. Children are to listen carefully and decide whether what you read is a friendship "fact" (something that is true). If so, they are to put a token in their milk carton. Pause after each statement to allow time for children to put in a token if they think the item is a fact.

FRIENDSHIP "FACTS"

- ► Friends never fight.
- ► Friends have to look exactly like you (same color of hair, skin, and so forth).
- ► Friends can forgive each other if they have had an argument.
- ► Friends can be older or younger than you are.
- ► You can have more than one good friend at the same time.
- ► Pets can make good friends.
- ► Friends sometimes have problems with each other.
- ► Your friend should always do what you want to do.
- ► Friends stay friends forever.
- ► Friends can do nice things for each other.
- ► Friends always like to do the same thing.

5. Elicit other examples from the children and continue as time permits, then discuss the Content and Personalization Questions.

Discussion

CONTENT QUESTIONS

1. How many tokens did you have in your carton? Were there some "facts" that were difficult to decide about? (Initiate discussion about the list of friendship facts and discuss opinions.)

2. Which of the items did you definitely feel weren't friendship facts? (Invite discussion, emphasizing that friendships do change over time, that friends can be older or younger and not look exactly alike, that you can have more than one good friend at a time, that friends don't always have to do what the other wants, and that there are times when friends don't get along.)

PERSONALIZATION QUESTIONS

1. What is the most important thing to you about your friends?

2. How can you be a better friend? How would you like your friends to be better friends to you?

3. What did you learn from this lesson that will help you in your friendships?

Follow-up Activity

Have children design friendship greeting cards that reflect some of the facts about friendships. Encourage children to give these to special friends.

Friends Come in All Shapes & Sizes

Developmental Perspective

During the middle childhood years, friendship patterns gradually become more rigid, making it difficult for outsiders to join an established group. The size of friendship networks also begins to decrease, and many children can be left out. Helping children expand their concept of friendship may help counteract their tendency to be rigid about these issues.

Objective

▷ To identify many different kinds of friends

Materials

▷ A large tagboard triangle, square, circle, and rectangle. On each shape, glue a picture of one of the following:

An animal

An elementary-age child

An older person

A child whose skin color is different from that of the majority of children in the group

▷ A copy of the Friends Come in All Shapes and Sizes–Worksheet (Handout 2) for each child

▷ Crayons, scissors, and glue for each child

▷ Several long sheets of butcher paper, labeled "Friends Come in All Shapes and Sizes."

Procedure

1. Introduce the lesson by holding up the large tagboard shapes with the pictures pasted on them. Indicate that the topic will be the many different kinds of friends people have. Engage children in a discussion about the types of friends represented in the pictures: pets, older friends, friends their own age, and friends of a different race or nationality. Ask children to think of other types of friends, such as friends of the same or a different sex, friends from a different country, friends who look different because they are taller or shorter or thinner or heavier, and so on.

2. Distribute the Friends Come in All Shapes and Sizes–Worksheet (Handout 2). Have children take out crayons and, in each shape, draw a picture of a different type of friend they have, based on examples from the previous discussion.

3. When children have finished drawing, have them cut around their shapes and take turns pasting them on one of the sheets of butcher paper to form group collages.

4. Allow time for children to look at the collages and share about their different types of friends, then discuss the Content and Personalization Questions.

Discussion

CONTENT QUESTIONS

1. Do all friends look alike?
2. Do all friends act alike?
3. Do all friends think alike?
4. Do you do different kinds of things with different kinds of friends?
5. Do you think it is important to have many different kinds of friends? If so, why?

PERSONALIZATION QUESTIONS

1. Do you have lots of different kinds of friends? (Invite sharing of examples.)
2. Can you think of a type of friend you don't have but would like to have? How could you become friends?

Follow-up Activity

Ask children to find a library book that illustrates different types of friendships and arrange a time when they can read their stories to the group.

Friends Come in All Shapes & Sizes

WORKSHEET–PAGE 1

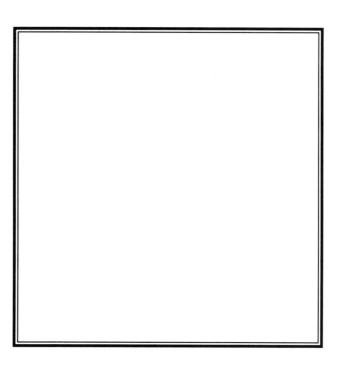

Friends Come in All Shapes & Sizes

WORKSHEET–PAGE 2

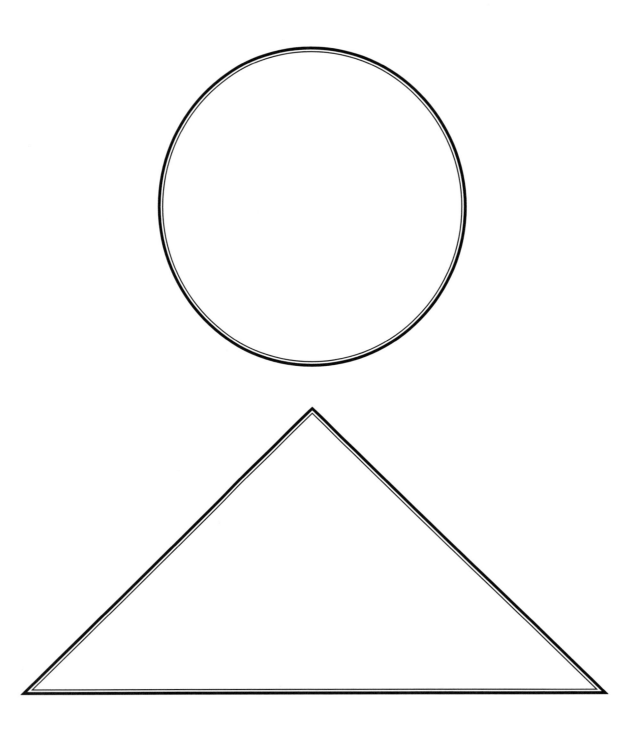

Circles of Friendship

Developmental Perspective

Socialization in the context of a peer group becomes a central issue for children this age. Acceptance in a group becomes increasingly important. Children need to understand that how they act in interpersonal situations can affect how they are treated by others. Recognizing positive friendship behaviors is an important part of their social development.

Objective

▷ To distinguish between positive and negative friendship behaviors

Materials

▷ Two hula hoops

▷ Two bean bags

▷ A copy of the Circles of Friendship–Positive and Negative Behaviors (Handout 3)

▷ Strips of tagboard and glue

▷ A 5 × 8–inch index card, crayons, and a safety pin for each child (optional)

▷ A shoe box labeled "Circles of Friendship" and several blank slips of paper (for the Follow-up Activity)

Procedure

1. Place the two hula hoops on the floor and explain that they are "circles of friendship." Next place the tagboard strips, on which you have glued the Circles of Friendship–Positive and Negative Behaviors (Handout 3), randomly on the floor around the hula hoops.

2. Divide children into two lines in front of the hula hoops. Give each line leader a bean bag. Explain that children in each line will take turns throwing the bean bag at one of the strips of paper around the hula hoop. When the bags land, the children are to walk over to it and pick up the closest strip. You will then read each strip aloud (or the children can, depending on reading level), and the children will decide if what is written represents a good friendship behavior. If so, they step into the "circle of friendship" next to their line. If not, they stand outside the circle. Then the next two players toss the bean bags, and the game continues in this manner until all children have had an opportunity to throw the bean bag and make a decision about whether or not to step into the circles.

3. Process the activity by asking the Content and Personalization Questions.

Discussion

CONTENT QUESTIONS

1. Was it difficult to decide which were friendship behaviors and which weren't? How did you know?

2. Which behaviors do you think will help you make and keep friends? (Make a list of these suggestions and keep them posted in the room so children can refer to them.)

PERSONALIZATION QUESTIONS

1. Do you think you practice more positive or more negative friendship behaviors? How do you feel about this?

2. When you are with someone who practices negative friendship behaviors, how do you feel? Do you enjoy playing with others who act this way?

3. Is there a friendship behavior you don't practice now that you would like to? If so, what is it and how can you learn it? (Optional: Children may draw a picture of the behavior they would like to practice on a 5 × 8–inch index card and wear it like a name tag as a reminder.)

Follow-up Activity

Invite children to practice some of the positive friendship behaviors identified in this lesson. As they do something positive, have them write it on a slip of paper and put it in the "Circles of Friendship" box. At the end of each day, draw the slips of paper out of the box and read the positive behaviors that were practiced.

Circles of Friendship

POSITIVE AND NEGATIVE BEHAVIORS

Leader note: Make one copy, then cut the items apart. Glue on separate strips of tagboard.

I like your shirt.

Can I please play?

Your jacket is ugly.

That was a great catch.

You missed a lot of problems.
You must be dumb.

I don't like you.

I want you to be my friend.

Let's ask her to play since
she's standing all alone.

You're really fun to play with.

Do you want to play your game first
and then we can play mine?

Shut up.

It's your turn to decide what we'll play.

You can't have that . . . it's mine.

I don't want to play that stupid game.

You cheat.

That's a stupid idea.

I won't play if you don't do
what I want to do.

Let's share.

Do you want to play with my new toy?

You have good ideas, so I hope
I get to work with you.

I'll never let you play with my things.

You run funny; I don't want
you on my team.

Don't play with him. He stinks.

Thanks for keeping my secret.

What's the Problem?

Developmental Perspective

Children at this age are beginning to take into account several aspects of a situation in solving a problem, but they need to learn how to clearly organize information and identify specific steps in the problem-solving process so they can effectively utilize these cognitive skills.

Objectives

▷ To learn to define problems clearly

▷ To identify steps in the problem-solving process

Materials

▷ Chalkboard

▷ A copy of the What's the Problem? Worksheet (Handout 4) and a pencil for each partnership

▷ A newsprint poster of the following "Rules For Brainstorming":

Work for as many ideas as possible.

Think of crazy, far-out ideas.

Don't rule out any ideas during the brainstorming process.

Piggy-back off of others' ideas.

Write down each idea.

▷ The following props: a jacket, a picture of a messy room, and three different kinds of candy bars

Procedure

1. Introduce the lesson by reading the following limerick to the children. Instruct them to listen carefully to see if they can identify the problem:

There was a young man named Fred
Who couldn't get out of his bed.
His bed was so high
It nearly touched the sky,
And Fred fell out on his head.

Elicit from children what they think Fred's problem was. Then write the problem on the chalkboard in the form of a question: "How could Fred get out of bed?"

2. Explain that the first step in solving a problem is to identify what the problem is. The second step is to brainstorm as many different ways to solve the problem as possible. Post the newsprint poster of the Rules for Brainstorming and review each rule. Then give children three or four minutes as a large group to brainstorm ways to solve Fred's problem. As they brainstorm, write their ideas on the chalkboard.

3. Next introduce the third step of the problem-solving process, which is to select the idea they think would work the best to solve the problem. Invite children to look at the list of ideas they brainstormed and discuss which ones they think would not work (and why). Ask others to agree or disagree with eliminating these ideas and draw a line through them as the majority of the children agree they won't work. Continue this process until the best solution has been determined.

4. Finally, introduce the last step of the problem-solving process, which is to make a plan and carry it out. Ask children to suggest a hypothetical plan for Fred, based on the agreed-upon solution.

5. Ask children to find a partner and give each partnership a copy of the What's the Problem? Worksheet (Handout 4) and a pencil. Explain that you will be giving them several problems to solve. Children should follow the steps in the problem-solving process to find a solution to each problem as you introduce it. Give help as necessary; allow sufficient time for children to arrive at a solution for one problem before proceeding to the next.

   ► Problem 1: Hold up the jacket. Have them imagine they were in the shopping center and lost the jacket.

   ► Problem 2: Hold up the picture of the messy room. Tell children to imagine this is their room and they have to clean it.

   ► Problem 3: Hold up the three candy bars. Tell children to imagine that they are in the candy store and they can only choose one.

6. After they have finished the worksheet, allow time for partners to share their solutions with the total group.

7. Process the activity by asking the Content and Personalization Questions.

Discussion

CONTENT QUESTIONS

1. Do you think using the steps in the problem-solving process helped you find a good solution to these problems? (Invite sharing.)

2. Which step of the process was the hardest for you to do? Which was the easiest?

3. How do you think you would find solutions if you didn't use this process?

PERSONALIZATION QUESTIONS

1. When you have a problem, how do you find a solution?

2. Do you think it would be helpful to use the problem-solving process with problems you have?

Follow-up Activity

Have children make up a limerick about a problem, similar to the one used
to introduce the lesson. Invite them to give their limerick to a partner, who should
apply the problem-solving process and arrive at a solution.

What's the Problem?

WORKSHEET—PAGE 1

Instructions: Use the problem-solving process to find an answer to each problem. Write your ideas in the spaces provided.

PROBLEM 1   **Step 1: What's the problem?**

_____

_____

_____

Step 2: Brainstorm different answers.

_____

_____

_____

Step 3: Choose the best idea.

_____

_____

Step 4: Make a plan.

_____

_____

_____

What's the Problem?

WORKSHEET—PAGE 2

PROBLEM 2   **Step 1: What's the problem?**

_____

_____

_____

Step 2: Brainstorm different answers.

_____

_____

_____

_____

Step 3: Choose the best idea.

_____

_____

Step 4: Make a plan.

_____

_____

_____

What's the Problem?

WORKSHEET—PAGE 3

PROBLEM 3   **Step 1: What's the problem?**

_____

_____

_____

Step 2: Brainstorm different answers.

_____

_____

_____

Step 3: Choose the best idea.

_____

_____

Step 4: Make a plan.

_____

_____

_____

Is That a Fact?

Developmental Perspective

Despite their increased ability to think logically, children often fail to distinguish between facts and assumptions. Failure to do so can result in misunderstandings and create problems in a number of different areas.

Objectives

▷ To differentiate between facts and assumptions

▷ To identify the negative consequences that can result from making assumptions

Materials

▷ Several pictures from magazines or photographs about which fact versus assumption statements can be formulated (for example, pictures of faces showing emotions, pictures of persons involved in some action but without a great deal of background detail)

▷ Paper and pencil for each child

▷ An audiotape player and a tape of children's music

Procedure

1. Display the magazine pictures or photographs selected, one by one, and ask children what they think the person is feeling and what they think might be happening. Then ask them to tell you a fact about the pictures, such as what color shirt a person is wearing, how many people are involved, or what actions they can see taking place.

2. Discuss the difference between a fact (something you can *prove* is true) versus an assumption (something you *think* is true). Elaborate on this concept so children understand that assumptions are just guesses about what might be happening and that it is very common for people to make assumptions without checking out the facts.

3. Next ask children to get out paper and pencil and number their papers 1–8. Indicate that you will be reading some short situations. Their task is to decide if what you read is a fact or an assumption and to write either an *F* for fact or an *A* for assumption on their papers.

   ▶ Situation 1: Justin is always talkative in the classroom in the morning. This morning he is very quiet. The teacher was talking to him outside the classroom door. Justin must be in trouble with the teacher. *(A)*

   ▶ Situation 2: Angelina usually does not sit with Stacey at lunch or play with her at recess. Today they sat together and talked and laughed the whole time. Angelina and Stacey are best friends. *(A)*

► Situation 3: Demetrius only eats cocoa crunchies for breakfast. When he got to the kitchen this morning, his father informed him that all the cereal was gone, so Demetrius refused to eat breakfast. *(F)*

► Situation 4: Marcus and Joey were seen fighting on the playground before school. Later in the day, Jasmine saw the two boys coming out of the principal's office. She is sure the boys won't be allowed to come to the school picnic next week. *(A)*

► Situation 5: You have looked all over for your new pencil. You had it in your desk just before you left the room to go to the library. You are sure you did not take it with you to the library. Your pencil is lost. *(F)*

► Situation 6: The teacher always smiles at you in the morning. Today she walked right past you in the hall and did not smile. You know she is angry with you. *(A)*

► Situation 7: You are almost late for the bus. When you get on, you notice that your friend Kareem is sitting with someone else. You are disappointed. *(F)*

► Situation 8: You put two quarters in your desk when you came to school this morning. Now the money is missing. You are sure Chad stole it, even though you didn't see him take it. *(A)*

4. After children have finished marking their papers, take each of the assumptions (1, 2, 4, 6, and 8) and discuss why they are assumptions and not facts. Then engage children in a discussion about the negative consequences that can occur when people make assumptions. For example, if you assume that someone stole your money and you accuse him or her of it, the person might be very angry and not be your friend again. Elicit other examples from the children.

5. Next ask children to quietly bring a chair to the front of the room. Place all chairs in a circle but remove one. Explain that you will play some music and that children will walk around the circle of chairs until the music stops. As soon as it stops, they need to find a chair and sit down. The child who is left standing will listen as the leader reads either a fact or an assumption from the following list. The child will state out loud what he or she thinks the statement is and why, and the others will have a chance to agree or disagree before the child goes back to the circle and the music starts again. The next child who is left standing when the music stops follows the same procedure, and the game continues until all facts and assumptions have been read.

IS THAT A FACT?

► Corn is a vegetable. *(F)*

► Cats are great pets. *(A)*

► This is a wonderful school. *(A)*

► Cows are animals. *(F)*

► Math is easy. *(A)*

► School lunches are good. *(A)*

   ► If someone is frowning, that person is angry. *(A)*

   ► Girls are smarter than boys. *(A)*

   ► Some dogs bite. *(F)*

   ► If a friend doesn't sit by you at lunch, he or she is mad at you. *(A)*

   ► It's hard to learn how to swim. *(A)*

   ► If you don't get invited to a party, it is because no one likes you. *(A)*

   ► Everyone gives valentines on Valentine's Day. *(A)*

   ► Losing a tooth is exciting. *(A)*

   ► If someone doesn't look at you, it means the person isn't your friend anymore. *(A)*

   ► An apple is a fruit. *(F)*

   ► Washington, D.C., is the capital of the United States. *(F)*

   ► Second graders are nicer than third graders. *(A)*

   ► Red is a color. *(F)*

   ► When the wind blows it means there will be a tornado. *(A)*

   ► If someone is mad at you today, the person will always be mad at you. *(A)*

6. Process the activity by asking the Content and Personalization Questions.

Discussion

CONTENT QUESTIONS

1. What is a fact?

2. How is a fact different from an assumption?

3. How can you change an assumption into a fact?

4. What are some of the bad things that can happen as a result of making assumptions?

PERSONALIZATION QUESTIONS

1. Think about a time when an assumption was made about you that was untrue. How did you feel, and what were the consequences?

2. Have you ever made an assumption and been right?

3. What can you do to avoid making assumptions that could be wrong?

4. How do you think that knowing the difference between a fact and an assumption might help you in your relationships with your friends? Your parents? Your teachers?

Follow-up Activity

Ask children to work in pairs and make up several examples of facts and assumptions. Pool all examples and play the musical chairs game again, using their examples.

Decisions, Decisions, Decisions

Developmental Perspective

Children are growing up in an increasingly complex society. Consequently, it is likely that as they mature they will be forced to make numerous decisions, many of which are more difficult and have more significant consequences than did those made by children in previous generations. Learning to evaluate decisions is a skill children must learn at an early age.

Objectives

▷ To identify decisions in everyday life

▷ To learn to evaluate decisions as good, fair, or poor

Materials

▷ A copy of the Decisions, Decisions, Decisions–Hunt Sheet (Handout 5) and a pencil for each child

Procedure

1. Introduce the lesson by explaining to children that they are going on a "decision hunt," but first they will need to tell you what a *decision* is. Discuss the fact that when you make a decision, you make up your mind about something–for example, deciding to listen when the teacher is talking instead of whispering to your neighbor. Emphasize that decisions can be good, fair, or poor.

2. Give a Decisions, Decisions, Decisions–Hunt Sheet (Handout 5) to each child and make sure each child has a pencil. Explain that children will be walking around the room to find others who can sign one of their spaces because they have made that decision. During the hunt there is to be no talking; children simply approach another child, hold out the paper, and the child either signs his or her name in a space or hands the paper back and shakes his or her head "no" if there is nothing he or she can sign. Tell children that they only need one signature per space, and when they have all the spaces signed they should sit down.

Leader note: Depending on children's reading level, you may need to read items aloud before beginning.

3. After all or most of the children have finished the hunt, discuss each of the decisions and ask children whether they think these were good, fair, or poor decisions and why. Emphasize the importance of looking at the *consequence* to help them evaluate the decision. Give an example: If you are very tired (consequence) because you stayed up long past your bedtime, was staying up a good decision? Elaborate on this concept and also on the fact that some decisions might be good for some children but bad for others. For example, it might be OK for a child who always gets all his or her spelling words right to watch television for a while instead of studying because he or she probably wouldn't need as much time to study. Elicit other examples from the children.

4. Process the activity by asking the Content and Personalization Questions.

Discussion

CONTENT QUESTIONS

1. Was it difficult for you to find other children to sign your sheet?

2. What are other examples of common decisions kids your age make?

3. How can you decide whether a decision is good, fair, or poor?

PERSONALIZATION QUESTIONS

1. When you make a decision, do you think about it carefully so it is the best decision you can make, or do you just decide quickly without thinking about it for too long?

2. Can you think of some decisions you have made quickly because they weren't really big decisions? (Elicit examples, such as which flavor of sucker to buy.)

3. Can you think of a decision you have made that has been very hard for you? What made it difficult?

Follow-up Activity

Invite children to take their hunt sheets home and ask parents or older siblings to help them think of other examples of decisions they regularly make. Ask children to discuss with others whether the decisions they usually make are good, fair, or poor.

Decisions, Decisions, Decisions

HUNT SHEET

Name: _____ Date: _____

Instructions: Walk around without talking. Hand your sheet to other children. If a person has made one or more of the decisions, he or she may sign those spaces on your sheet. You need to get only one signature for each space.

Name

1. Decided to eat cereal instead of eggs for breakfast

   _____

2. Decided to tease your sister or brother instead of being nice

   _____

3. Decided to go home when your mother called you instead of playing outside a little longer

   _____

4. Decided to watch television after school instead of picking up your room as you were told to do

   _____

5. Decided to go to bed when it was time without arguing with your parents about it

   _____

6. Decided to share your toys with your brother or sister without anyone asking you to do that

   _____

7. Decided to talk back to your mother when she asked you to pick up your toys

   _____

8. Decided to wander away in the store even though your parents said to stay beside them

   _____

Other Options

Developmental Perspective

Because children at this stage of development are concrete thinkers, they often take things very literally, and it is difficult for them to consider other options. This limitation in their cognitive ability affects them socially, emotionally, and academically. Teaching them to see alternative ways of looking at situations is a critical part of their cognitive development.

Objectives

▷ To identify options

▷ To learn how considering options can affect feelings and behavior

Materials

▷ Three puppets

▷ A roll of masking tape

▷ Paper and crayons for each child

Procedure

1. Introduce this lesson by putting on a brief puppet play for the children. Introduce the characters: Rigid Richard, Absolutely Annabel, and Other Options Oliver. The puppets are trying to decide what to do inside since it is raining and they can't play outside. Rigid Richard says that he wants to play with Legos, and Absolutely Annabel says she wants to color. They both argue over which idea is best. Then Other Options Oliver steps in and says that there are lots of other things they could do besides color or play with Legos. He suggests things such as making a castle out of boxes, putting on a puppet show for their friends, or making monsters out of playdough. The other two puppets just look at Oliver and say that they hadn't thought of other ideas like that.

2. Discuss with children the fact that we sometimes look at things in an either-or way instead of seeing other *options*. Use the following example: Your teacher doesn't ask you to be the classroom helper, so you think he doesn't consider you to be a good helper. If he had selected you, you would think that he sees you as a good helper. Ask children to identify other reasons the teacher may not have selected you to be the helper: Maybe you had been the helper last week or the teacher picked a girl last time so he wanted to pick a boy this time. Use another example: A friend doesn't ask you to a birthday party. You think that if you are asked, it means that this friend likes you, and if you aren't asked, that this friend doesn't like you. Elicit ideas from the children about other options/ways of thinking about this—for example, the friend could only invite a few kids or the friend invited you last year so decided to invite someone else this year. Discuss

what could happen if you look at the situation in an either-or way: You might feel very sad, or you might not speak to the friend (and then the friend wouldn't speak to you and you could get into a fight). If you also considered other options, you probably wouldn't be as sad or as mad.

3. Put a long strip of masking tape on the floor and tell children that this represents a *continuum*. Explain that a continuum can show a variety of options: At one end is one position, at the other end is a different position, and in between are many other options. Ask for two volunteers to come and stand beside the line. Indicate that one end of the line represents *always disobey* and the other end of the line represents *never disobey*. The middle of the line represents *sometimes disobey*, and in between sometimes and never/always are *disobey quite a lot* and *obey quite a lot*. Then read the following situation:

   > Last night Keisha's mom was out on a date, and Keisha and her brother disobeyed their mother. They weren't supposed to eat candy (but they did), and they were supposed to go to bed at 9:00 (but they convinced the baby-sitter to let them stay up until midnight).

   Ask the two volunteers to think about whether Keisha and her brother *always disobey, never disobey,* or if they think their behavior is somewhere in between. Have the volunteers actually take a position on the line. After they have positioned themselves, discuss where they are standing and why. Emphasize the fact that in this situation there are not just two ways of thinking about this situation (always or never): There are other options.

4. Read the next situation, and this time ask for four volunteers. Instruct the group to listen to the following situation:

   > Samuel's dad wanted him to spend the weekend, but Samuel had a scout camp out on Friday night until noon on Saturday. Samuel wanted to see his dad, but he also really wanted to go on the scout overnight trip. What options can you think of for Samuel?

   Designate one end of the line as *go with his dad* and the other end as *go with the scouts*. Ask volunteers to take a stand on the line that represents any option, including the two identified. After all the volunteers are in place, have them state their positions. As you debrief, point out the optional ways of looking at the situation.

5. Have children take out paper and crayons. Ask them to draw a cartoon that depicts a problem situation and the optional ways of looking at it. They may want to use conversation bubbles (as in cartoons) to help get their points across.

6. Allow time for children to share their cartoons, then discuss the Content and Personalization Questions.

Discussion

CONTENT QUESTIONS

1. As you were drawing your cartoons, was it hard for you to think of optional ways of looking at the situation?
2. Do you think it is important to identify optional viewpoints? Why or why not?
3. What are some of the bad things that can happen if you don't look at all the options in a situation?

PERSONALIZATION QUESTIONS

1. Do you usually think of other options, or are you an "either-or" kid?
2. Have you ever had any bad feelings or acted badly because you didn't identify options or other ways of thinking about a situation? (Invite sharing.)
3. What did you learn from this lesson that might help you in the future?

Follow-up Activity

Keep the masking tape on the floor and as incidents arise ask children to identify options on the line to help them get a better perspective on the situation.

the **PASSPORT** PROGRAM

GRADE 3

Self-Development
ACTIVITY
1 Who I Am, How I Act
2 Being Perfectly Perfect
3 One, Two, Three, Me
4 Who Me? Yes You!

Emotional Development
ACTIVITY
1 How Do I Feel?
2 Fixing Our Feelings
3 Being Anxious
4 Feeling Fine, a Little Fine, or Not So Fine

Social Development
ACTIVITY
1 Boys Do, Girls Do
2 Together Is Better
3 Find a Friend
4 They Didn't Choose Me

Cognitive Development
ACTIVITY
1 Big, Little, or In-Between Decisions
2 What Happens If?
3 Solve It
4 Thinking Makes It So

Who I Am, How I Act

Developmental Perspective

One of the critical tasks during middle childhood is developing standards and expectations for one's behavior, as well as strategies for controlling behavior. As they mature, children begin to incorporate their behavioral standards into their self-concept. Because they are still in the concrete thinking stage, it is easy for them to equate their self-worth with their behavior. This equation can result in a negative self-concept. It is important for children to develop the ability to see that they can change their behavior, but that how they act is not a reflection of their worth as a person.

Objective

▷ To learn that how one acts does not determine self-worth

Materials

▷ Chalkboard

▷ Three tin cans per child with a blank stick-on label for each can (children can bring cans from home, or you may use library pocket cards)

▷ Ten tokens (pennies, paper clips, soda bottle caps) per child

Procedure

1. Introduce the lesson by having the children close their eyes and think about a time when they behaved very well. Invite them to give examples of what those good behaviors were and write them on the chalkboard. Then ask them to close their eyes and think about a time when they behaved badly. Again, ask them for examples of what these behaviors were and write them on the board.

2. Next distribute the tin cans (or library pocket cards) and the tokens to each child. Ask children to write the word *good* on one can, the word *bad* on another, and *sort of good/sort of bad* on the third. Indicate that you will be reading some scenarios. After you read each one, children are to put a penny or token in the can that best describes how they would classify that behavior (as good, bad, or sort of good/sort of bad).

WHO I AM, HOW I ACT—SCENARIOS

▶ You go over to your friend's house after school. He wants to play something that you don't, so you tell him you feel sick and go home.

▶ You are invited to a birthday party. You don't like the kid very well, but you go anyway and give her a nice present.

▶ You see one of your friends fall off her bike. You walk over and help her pick up her bike and ask her if she is hurt.

> ► You are on the playground during recess. A fifth grader comes up and tries to take a ball away from one of your classmates. You kick the fifth grader in the leg and yell at him to go away.

> ► You and your cousin are going to the movies with your aunt. Your aunt says you can't have any popcorn because it will spoil your supper. You pout and tell her that you didn't want to go to the stupid movie with her anyway.

> ► You heard your mother say that your classmate's dad is in jail. You go to school the next day and tell everyone else in your reading group.

> ► You got all your spelling words right, but the girl sitting across from you missed some. You ask her why she missed so many.

> ► Your grandmother is sick. You make her a card and pick some flowers from the garden to take to her.

> ► You are going to visit your dad and stepmother this weekend. When you get there, your stepsister asks if she can play with your video game. You say no and tell her to go away.

3. After all of the scenarios have been read, ask children to count the tokens in each can. Have them indicate their numbers and record these on the board in order to arrive at a grand total for each can. Discuss Content Questions 1–3.

4. Read the following story, then discuss the remaining Content Questions and the Personalization Questions.

WHO I AM, HOW I ACT–STORY

> Joshua had ridden his bike over to his friend Antonio's house. Shortly after Joshua got there, he and Antonio got into a fight because Antonio wouldn't let Joshua use his rollerblades. Joshua called Antonio some bad names, and Antonio told his stepmother. She told Joshua that he couldn't play at their house if he acted like that. Joshua got mad and stuck his tongue out at her, and she said that he would have to leave. On the way out the door, he kicked the rollerblades and slammed the door.

> Instead of going right home, Joshua rode around the block and stopped to play in the park. He lost track of the time, and when he finally did go home his dad was very angry. He had called Antonio's house, and when he found out that Joshua had been sent home, he was upset about that and worried because Joshua hadn't come straight home.

> Joshua's dad sent him to his room and told him to think about the things he had done. Joshua didn't want to go to his room, so he started to argue with his dad. But his dad held up his hand, told him to stop arguing, and said they would talk about the situation when Joshua calmed down.

Joshua reluctantly went to his room. After a while, his dad came in to see him. He sat down beside Joshua on the bed and said that it sounded like Joshua had had a bad day, with lots of different frustrations. His dad explained that sometimes when kids are frustrated, they don't know what to do about it, so the feelings just build up and sometimes kids act out like Joshua did. Joshua agreed and started to cry. "I'm always doing bad things; I'm just a bad kid," cried Joshua. "No, you're not a bad kid, Joshua," said his dad. "Sometimes you *act* bad, and you do mean or unkind things. Sometimes you don't cooperate or follow the rules, but that doesn't mean you are a bad kid. It means that you need to work on your behavior and make some changes so you don't do those bad things. It's also important for you to learn some good ways to handle your frustrations," said Joshua's dad.

Joshua thought about everything his dad had said, and then he asked, "But do you still love me when I do those bad things?" "Yes," said his dad. "I love you a lot, but sometimes I don't like what you do. Even if you do these bad things, you are still a lovable kid. But do you think you would be happier if you could change your behavior?" Joshua thought about this and said _____.
(Ask children what they think Joshua would say and why.)

Discussion

CONTENT QUESTIONS

1. How did you decide which behaviors were *good, bad,* or *sort of good/sort of bad?*
2. Did everyone in this group agree on which behaviors were *good, bad,* and *sort of good/sort of bad?*
3. For those behaviors you decided were *bad,* what would have been a better choice? (Review those scenarios and discuss optional behaviors.)
4. What were some of the bad things that Joshua did?
5. Do you think Joshua was a bad kid because he acted that way?
6. Do you think Joshua's parents should stop loving him because he acted like that?
7. What did Joshua's dad tell Joshua about his behavior? How did his dad feel about him?

PERSONALIZATION QUESTIONS

1. Have you ever done things that you or other people didn't like?
2. Did this make you a bad kid, or did it mean that you were still a good kid but your behavior needed to change?
3. If you behave badly, how do you feel? Is there anything you can do to change how you behave? (Invite sharing of ideas, but continue to emphasize that children are not bad kids if they behave badly.)

Follow-up Activity

Have children develop and perform puppet plays or skits that emphasize the fact that children are good and lovable kids regardless of their behavior and to show that bad behavior can be changed.

Being Perfectly Perfect

Developmental Perspective

Because children are still in the concrete thinking stage, they look at things dichotomously. As a result, they tend to see themselves as successes or failures, perfect or imperfect. It is important to help them see that perfect persons don't exist. Rather, they need to be able to accept themselves, with their strengths as well as limitations, and work on overcoming their limitations when possible.

Objectives

▷ To learn that nobody is perfect

▷ To learn to accept oneself as less than perfect

Materials

▷ None

Procedure

1. Introduce the idea of being perfect: Do children know anybody who is perfect? Can anyone do everything perfectly all the time? Are there any bad things that come from trying to be perfect? Any good things?

2. Read the following story aloud, then ask the Content and Personalization Questions.

PRISCILLA'S PERFECT TEA PARTY
by David Martino

Once there was a little girl named Priscilla. Now Priscilla was a "just so" kind of girl because she had to have everything just so— her hair had to be just so, her clothes had to be just so, she put her toys in exactly the same spot every night, and she never made a mess at the dinner table. In fact, one night she was eating peas, and one happened to fall off her fork and onto the table, and Priscilla cried and cried for hours. Every night before bed, she had to follow exactly the same routine—take a bath (wash legs first, then arms, then face—just so) and put on freshly folded pajamas. Then she would hop into bed, pull one sheet up, smooth it out, pull the blanket up, smooth it out, before settling her combed hair (35 brushstrokes) on her prefluffed pillow. Then her mother would recite the same three stories, in exactly the same order, and would give Priscilla a kiss (left cheek) before turning out the lights. Priscilla would sigh—another day, just so, and tomorrow, so much to do to make it just so, too.

When morning came, Priscilla would go over in her mind all the things she had to do for the day. Sometimes, the web she built of phrases like "I MUST do that" or "I SHOULD do this" would get so sticky that it was hard for her to get out of bed. Today was the day of the tea party—and not just any tea party, a tea party, a PERFECT tea party. Priscilla was new in the neighborhood, and everything HAD to be perfect. "It HAS to be perfect because I HAVE to find the perfect friend!" said Priscilla. She spent hours setting everything up. She washed her best tea service—not once but twice. In fact, she washed one of the cups so hard that it broke. Priscilla cried and cried, and told her mother to tell everyone that the tea party was canceled, but her mother convinced her that a cup from her old tea service would do just as well.

Finally everything was "just so"—perfect in fact—and Priscilla didn't even want to breathe because she thought it might spoil things. The polished teapot reflected a bright light onto the beautiful white tablecloth and made the blue-edged cups look like little ships on a silvery sea. The doorbell rang. Priscilla took one last look at herself in the mirror, straightened a pleat on her dress, picked off a piece of invisible lint from her shirt, and walked calmly to the door. When she opened it, two boys and a girl tumbled in, chasing a muddy football. "Hi, we're your neighbors," said one of the boys, and he stuck out his hand, which was covered with dirt and day-old chocolate. Priscilla jumped back. The girl tossed Priscilla the muddy football, but Priscilla just screamed and threw her hands in the air. The football made a big brown stain on her freshly pressed white dress. Priscilla was about to go crying into her bedroom when the doorbell rang again. She opened the door, and four more children— two boys and two girls—rushed in. "Hey!" one of them shouted, but it was obvious that they were playing a game of tag and were pretty busy avoiding one another. Priscilla took one look at their dirty, torn clothes, tattered sneakers, and grubby faces, and wanted to scream. But instead, she regained as much composure as she could and yelled, "Tea . . . is . . . SERVED!"

The children stopped what they were doing, looked at Priscilla, and sat down. But even before they were all seated, someone had already spilled a cup of tea all over the carpet that Priscilla had just vacuumed. No one even bothered to get a rag. The children's muddy hands made brown marks all over the cups and pot that Priscilla had just shined. No one had any manners, no one did what he or she was supposed to do, no one was being at all perfect, so Priscilla, who had reached her boiling point, shouted at the top of her lungs, "EVERYBODY OUT!" They all stared at her, then she said again, "You heard me, EVERYBODY OUT!" And then Priscilla started crying and ran to her room.

After some time and many tears, Priscilla ventured out of her room. She went to the tea party room, and one little girl was seated at the table, drinking some tea. Priscilla walked to the table, sat down, and with swollen red eyes asked, "How come you didn't go with the other children?"

"Do you want me to?" asked the girl.

"Oh, no, please stay," pleaded Priscilla, then she started to sob softly.

"What's wrong?" asked the girl.

"Oh, my party. I wanted everything to be so perfect, and, and, just look at this mess! I'm a complete failure!" Priscilla started to cry again.

"Well, this party was a bomb, but that doesn't mean you're a failure," said the girl, who was sort of laughing but not in a mean way.

"Everyone must HATE me!" sobbed Priscilla.

"Oh, no," said the girl, "It's not that they didn't like you. They just didn't like the party, that's all."

"But everything was so, so PERFECT!" said Priscilla.

"That's the problem," smiled the girl. "What's the use of having something perfect if you can't mess it up sometimes?"

"But if it's not perfect, then I won't be able to find things, and I won't be able to know what to expect, and . . ."

"And you might spend a lot less time worrying about what SHOULD be and a lot more time thinking about what CAN be," said the girl. Priscilla considered this, and for the first time that day, a little smile danced on her lips. "My name's Amy," said the girl. "Good to meetcha."

"How about some tea?" asked Priscilla.

"I'd love some," replied Amy.

As Priscilla was pouring, a big splash of tea splattered over her cup and onto the tablecloth. Priscilla looked at the spot and started laughing and laughing. Amy laughed right along with her. Priscilla went on to make friends with many of the children who had been to her not-so-perfect tea party. They taught her how to live and enjoy life, and she taught them how to organize themselves and how to respect other people. Priscilla would never forget her tea party, where she became a little less perfect and a lot more happy.

Discussion

CONTENT QUESTIONS

1. What happened when Priscilla tried to make everything perfect?
2. Did you think she or others had fun at her tea party? Why or why not?
3. What did Amy teach Priscilla about having to be perfect?

PERSONALIZATION QUESTIONS

1. Have you ever gotten upset with yourself if you didn't do something perfectly?
2. Do you think there is something wrong with you if you aren't perfect?
3. Do you think you are still a good kid, even if you don't do things perfectly?

Follow-up Activity

As a group, create a poem about being perfect or imperfect. An example follows:

My father sent me to the store
to buy macaroni, nothing more.
But when I saw the candy
it looked so dandy
that I knew I had to buy it
before walking out the door.

One, Two, Three, Me

Developmental Perspective

During these middle childhood years, children's self-understanding continues to develop, and their concepts of self become more integrated. One of the critical self-acceptance tasks is to develop a relatively stable and comprehensive self-understanding, including awareness of "me" and "not me."

Objective

▷ To identify characteristics of self, including strengths and weaknesses

Materials

▷ Three empty cereal boxes for each child (children can bring boxes from home, or you may use manila envelopes if boxes are not available)

▷ Construction paper, magazines, scissors, crayons, and glue for each child

Procedure

1. Give each child three cereal boxes, scissors, glue, crayons, and a sheet of construction paper. Ask children to cut three strips of construction paper and glue one on each box. Then ask them to label the boxes as follows: *things I like, things I am good at,* and *things I am not so good at.*

2. Distribute magazines and additional sheets of construction paper to children and ask them to cut pictures out of magazines or draw pictures to represent at least five things they like (for example, things they like to eat; things they like to do; toys, games, animals, or books they like) and put them in the box labeled *things I like.*

3. When they have finished with *things I like,* have them find five pictures of *things I am good at* and five pictures of *things I am not so good at* and put these in the other two boxes.

4. Divide into groups of three and have children share their boxes, then discuss the Content and Personalization Questions.

Discussion

CONTENT QUESTIONS

1. Which was easiest: thinking of things you like, things you are good at, or things you are not so good at?

2. Were some of the things you shared similar to things other group members shared? What were some of the things that were different?

PERSONALIZATION QUESTIONS

1. Of all the things you do well, what are you the most proud of?

2. Of all the things you don't do so well, which one do you think you can most easily change? How do you think you will do that?

3. What does it mean about you if there are some things you are not so good at?

4. What do you like best about yourself? What do you think others like best about you?

Follow-up Activity

Have children keep the boxes and continue to add new things to them for a week or two. Schedule another time for them to share what they have added to the boxes.

Who Me? Yes You!

Developmental Perspective

As children begin to compare themselves to others in terms of such things as achievement, appearance, and group acceptance, they may become self-critical and struggle with self-acceptance. Children who grow up in dysfunctional family settings often receive very little positive reinforcement or support and therefore need practice accepting compliments and identifying good things about themselves.

Objectives

▷ To learn to accept compliments

▷ To identify personal strengths

Materials

▷ One Who Me? Yes You! Game Board (Handout 1) per child

▷ One game piece (penny, paper clip, soda bottle cap) for each child

▷ Paper, crayons, and scissors (for the Follow-up Activity)

Procedure

1. Introduce the lesson by asking children to think of one nice thing they can say about the person sitting beside them. After a minute of think-time, have them give this compliment to the other child. Ask children how they felt about accepting a compliment and hearing something nice about themselves.

2. Next give each child a Who Me? Yes You! Game Board (Handout 1) and a game piece. Explain that you will be reading some statements, and if a statement applies, children should move their pieces one space on the game board. If they do not think the statement applies to them, they should stay on the same spot. Children will move their pieces around the circle until all statements have been read.

3. Read the following compliments, one at a time. Allow children time to move their game pieces around the circle.

WHO ME? YES YOU! COMPLIMENTS

▶ You have a great smile.

▶ You are a fast worker.

▶ You are a very good reader.

▶ You cooperate well.

▶ You get along well with everyone.

▶ You do a good job picking up your toys and your room.

▶ You are a very good speller.

> ► You are a good swimmer.
> ► You do nice things for other people.
> ► You are a good leader.
> ► You are a nice kid to have around.
> ► You have pretty hair.
> ► You are a fast runner.
> ► You are honest (tell the truth).
> ► You have a good imagination.
> ► You draw or paint well.
> ► You aren't afraid to try new things.
> ► You are a good eater (not picky).
> ► You are fun to play with.
> ► You are a good singer.
> ► You are a smart kid.
> ► You play fair.
> ► You say kind things to others and don't call them names.
> ► You are a cute kid.

4. Process the activity by discussing the Content and Personalization Questions.

Discussion

CONTENT QUESTIONS

1. Was it easy or hard to know if these compliments applied to you?
2. How did you know if these compliments were true for you?

PERSONALIZATION QUESTIONS

1. Has anyone ever given you any of these compliments before? If so, how did you feel when this occurred?
2. Do you think you are bragging if you talk about your personal strengths? (Emphasize the difference between acknowledging your strengths and bragging about them in a way that puts you up and puts others down.)
3. When you have done something that you are pleased about, do you give yourself a compliment? If not, why do you think you don't?
4. Do you think you are sometimes harder on yourself than others are? In other words, do you think others see your strengths but you have a hard time seeing them yourself?
5. Based on the compliments that were true for you, what are some of your personal strengths?

Follow-up Activity

Invite children to make a banner of their strengths. Display the banner in the room.

Who Me? Yes You!

GAME BOARD

Instructions: If a statement is true for you, move your game piece one space on the board. If it is not true, stay where you are. When all the statements have been read, the game ends.

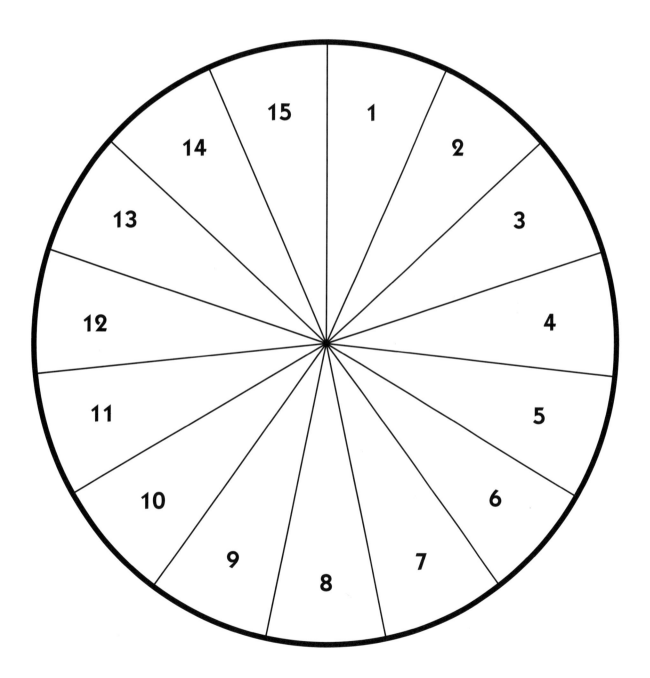

How Do I Feel?

Developmental Perspective

Although children this age are much better at recognizing a wide range of feelings than they were when they were in preschool, it is nevertheless important to continue to help them learn to identify feelings, understand that there are various ways to express them, and recognize that everyone doesn't necessarily feel the same way about each event. The skills developed at this age serve as an important building block in the emotional maturation process.

Objectives

▷ To learn to identify feelings

▷ To learn that people have different feelings about the same event

Materials

▷ Twelve blown-up balloons on strings. With a marker, write one of the following words on each balloon: *excited, disappointed, worried, angry, sad, grouchy, lonely, scared, upset, happy, confused, furious.*

▷ Twelve volunteers from the group to hold the balloons and one volunteer to be the recorder. If the group is smaller, use fewer people and have each one take more than one balloon.

▷ One How Do I Feel? Recorder Sheet (Handout 2)

▷ One green balloon on a string

▷ Chalkboard (for the Follow-up Activity)

Procedure

1. Explain that children will be participating in an activity designed to help them learn more about feelings. Ask for 12 volunteers to help with the activity.

2. Give each volunteer one or more balloons, depending on how many participate. Have the volunteers stand in front of the room with their balloons. Review the feeling word on each child's balloon and make sure everyone understands what each word means.

3. Instruct the volunteers that they are to listen carefully as you read the following situations. Then when you hold up the green balloon, they are to hold their balloons in the air and move out in front of the line if the word describes how they would feel in this situation. Instruct the recorder to look at the words on the balloons of volunteers who step in front of the line and to circle all these words on the How Do I Feel? Recorder Sheet (Handout 2). Read each situation, following this procedure.

HOW DO I FEEL? SITUATIONS

> ► Situation 1: You forgot to study your spelling words, and the test is today.
>
> ► Situation 2: You got invited to spend the night at a friend's house.
>
> ► Situation 3: You had to stay in for recess.
>
> ► Situation 4: You lost your lunch box.
>
> ► Situation 5: You forgot where you were supposed to go after school.
>
> ► Situation 6: You got in trouble because you didn't pick up your toys.
>
> ► Situation 7: You couldn't find anybody to play with after school.
>
> ► Situation 8: You are going to a new baby-sitter tonight after school.
>
> ► Situation 9: Someone in your class stole your book bag.
>
> ► Situation 10: You are going to your grandparents' house for the weekend.
>
> ► Situation 11: You didn't get to bed very early last night, and you didn't want to get up this morning.
>
> ► Situation 12: When you walked out the door this morning, a strange man started to follow you to school.

4. Process the activity by asking the Content and Personalization Questions.

Discussion

CONTENT QUESTIONS

1. Ask the recorder to read the words circled for the first situation, about forgetting to study. Ask children if anyone would have had any different feelings about this than the ones identified. Follow this same procedure for the other situations.

2. Was it difficult to identify feelings for these situations?

3. Why do you suppose there was more than one feeling that described most (or all) of these situations?

PERSONALIZATION QUESTIONS

1. Have you felt some of these same feelings in other situations? (Invite sharing.)

2. If you feel one way about a situation, and your friend or your parent feels another way, how can you tell that he or she doesn't feel the same way you do? (Invite children to give examples.)

3. What did you learn about feelings today?

Follow-up Activity

Have children find a partner. Each partnership will meet at the end of the day to describe two actual events and to share how they felt about them. Invite sharing with the total group and record feeling words on the chalkboard to help develop a feelings vocabulary.

How Do I Feel?

RECORDER SHEET–PAGE 1

SITUATION 1	Excited	Disappointed	Worried	Angry
	Sad	Grouchy	Lonely	Scared
	Upset	Happy	Confused	Furious
SITUATION 2	Excited	Disappointed	Worried	Angry
	Sad	Grouchy	Lonely	Scared
	Upset	Happy	Confused	Furious
SITUATION 3	Excited	Disappointed	Worried	Angry
	Sad	Grouchy	Lonely	Scared
	Upset	Happy	Confused	Furious
SITUATION 4	Excited	Disappointed	Worried	Angry
	Sad	Grouchy	Lonely	Scared
	Upset	Happy	Confused	Furious
SITUATION 5	Excited	Disappointed	Worried	Angry
	Sad	Grouchy	Lonely	Scared
	Upset	Happy	Confused	Furious
SITUATION 6	Excited	Disappointed	Worried	Angry
	Sad	Grouchy	Lonely	Scared
	Upset	Happy	Confused	Furious

How Do I Feel?

RECORDER SHEET–PAGE 2

SITUATION 7	Excited	Disappointed	Worried	Angry
	Sad	Grouchy	Lonely	Scared
	Upset	Happy	Confused	Furious
SITUATION 8	Excited	Disappointed	Worried	Angry
	Sad	Grouchy	Lonely	Scared
	Upset	Happy	Confused	Furious
SITUATION 9	Excited	Disappointed	Worried	Angry
	Sad	Grouchy	Lonely	Scared
	Upset	Happy	Confused	Furious
SITUATION 10	Excited	Disappointed	Worried	Angry
	Sad	Grouchy	Lonely	Scared
	Upset	Happy	Confused	Furious
SITUATION 11	Excited	Disappointed	Worried	Angry
	Sad	Grouchy	Lonely	Scared
	Upset	Happy	Confused	Furious
SITUATION 12	Excited	Disappointed	Worried	Angry
	Sad	Grouchy	Lonely	Scared
	Upset	Happy	Confused	Furious

Fixing Our Feelings

Developmental Perspective

In the normal course of growing up, children experience all sorts of feelings, both positive and negative. In contemporary society, more and more children are being exposed to disruptive family situations or other situations that evoke negative emotions. It is very important to help children learn ways to deal with these negative feelings so they don't become overwhelmed or discouraged.

Objective

▷ To learn positive ways to cope with hurtful feelings

Materials

▷ Paper and pencil for each child (for the Follow-up Activity)

Procedure

1. Introduce this activity by explaining that we have all sorts of feelings. Some of those feelings are *positive feelings* that we like to have, and some are *negative feelings* that we don't like to have. Ask children to give you some examples of both kinds of feelings. Indicate that you will be reading a story and that you would like them to identify the feelings of the main character, Sad Susanna.

2. Read the following story aloud, then discuss the Content and Personalization Questions.

FIXING OUR FEELINGS–STORY

It was Saturday morning. Normally, Susanna, age 8, liked to sleep in on Saturdays. But not today. She woke up very early and had already finished her breakfast when her stepfather came downstairs. Usually on Saturdays Susanna liked to stay in her pajamas and watch cartoons, but not this morning. As soon as she finished breakfast, she raced upstairs and got dressed. She put on the new sweatshirt and jeans she had gotten for her birthday, and she brushed her hair and tied it with one of her favorite ribbons. Next she packed her suitcase: some clothes, her night light, her book, and her teddy bear. She carried her bag downstairs and put it beside the front door. Then she settled down in a chair next to the window to wait for her dad to come pick her up.

Pretty soon Susanna got tired of waiting, so she went to the kitchen for a snack. She looked at the clock. It said 9:00. "Dad should be here any minute," Susanna thought. She took her snack back to the living room and kept looking down the street, hoping that any minute she would see her dad's car. More time passed, and Susanna started to get worried. "What if he had an accident?" she thought. She went back to the kitchen to look at the clock, and by this time it was 9:30. She went upstairs and asked her mother if she could call her dad to find out if he was on his way. "Susanna, your dad is always late when he is coming to pick you up. He just doesn't come very often, so you probably don't remember that he's never on time. Why don't you go watch some cartoons. That will help the time go by faster."

So Susanna sat down to watch cartoons, but she still kept going to the window every few minutes to check to see if her dad was coming down the street. Each time she looked, she didn't see his car, and she was getting more and more upset.

After her favorite cartoon show was over, Susanna went back and sat by the window again. This time she was crying. She had been so excited to see her dad because he didn't come to get her very often. She didn't understand why he didn't come. She was scared that something bad had happened to him, and she didn't know what to do.

Susanna's mother found her crying in front of the window and told Susanna she would call. Susanna stood by the phone while her mom called and talked to Susanna's stepmother. When her mom hung up, she said to Susanna, "I'm sorry, honey, but your dad forgot that this was the weekend he was coming to get you." "Then why can't he come and get me now since you called and let him know?" cried Susanna. "Susanna, I don't think he will come. He took your stepbrother on a camping trip this weekend." Mom put her arms around Susanna and held her while she cried and told her she was sorry. She asked Susanna what she could do to help her, and Susanna said she didn't know. She felt so sad. She kept thinking, "Why would Dad forget to come and get me? Why did he take my stepbrother on a camping trip and not even think about me? Doesn't he love me anymore?"

Pretty soon she fell asleep because she had been crying so hard. When she woke up she went to find her mother. She told her mother that she was going to write her dad a letter and tell him how she felt. Her mother said she thought that was a good idea and that it might help Susanna feel a little better. Susanna wasn't sure it would help, but she did go to her room and write the letter. She told her dad that she felt bad because he had forgotten about her and wondered if he loved her stepbrother more, since he took him camping. She said that she was mad because he hadn't sent her a birthday card, and she didn't understand why he didn't want to see her.

After she wrote the letter, she felt a tiny bit better because she had let some of her feelings out. She went downstairs and asked her mom if they could bake cookies, since this was one of her favorite things to do. After the cookies were baked, Mom asked her if she would like to go with her to take some cookies to Mrs. Beasley, who was Susanna's special friend at the nursing home. Mrs. Beasley was so glad to see her, but she noticed that Susanna didn't look as happy as she usually did when she came to visit. Susanna told her about her disappointment, and Mrs. Beasley gave her a big hug and said, "Sometimes it is hard to understand why people do the things they do, Susanna. You just have to remember that lots of people love you and want to be with you, and that just because your dad didn't come doesn't mean you're not a lovable kid. You can't help it that he didn't come, but you can tell him how you feel and you can try to do some things to help yourself feel better, which is what you have done this afternoon."

After Susanna and her mother left Mrs. Beasley, Susanna felt just a little bit better. She went home and played outside with her friend, which helped her stop thinking so much about her dad. By the time she went to bed, she still felt sad, but she knew that she just had to learn how to handle her disappointment. She still hoped he would come to see her soon.

Discussion

Content Questions

1. Why was Susanna sad?
2. What other feelings besides *sad* did Susanna have?
3. How did Susanna try to help herself feel better? Did these things work?

Personalization Questions

1. Have you ever had a situation similar to Susanna's? If so, did you feel the same way?
2. If you haven't had a situation like this, have you had some of the same feelings? Can you share a time when you felt sad? Disappointed? Upset?
3. When you have feelings like this, what do you do to try and help yourself feel better? Do you think any of the ideas that worked for Susanna could work for you?

Follow-up Activity

Have children write their own stories about a sad experience and how they "fixed" their feelings.

Being Anxious

Developmental Perspective

Children at this age are very eager to please their teachers, and they fear disapproval. Because their thinking at this stage of development is very concrete, it is common for them to assume that their teachers either do or do not like them. This evaluation is usually based on one act of misbehavior or one poor performance; they don't readily understand that approval or disapproval is generally not based on isolated incidents. They also are afraid of punishment from teachers. Because their feelings vocabularies are not always well developed at this age, children may show their anxieties in stomachaches and resistance about going to school.

Objective

▷ To develop skills in understanding and dealing with anxiety associated with disapproval

Materials

▷ Chalkboard

▷ One 15 × 4–inch tagboard strip per child. At one end of the strip, draw or place a sticker of a happy face; at the other end, a sad face.

▷ Eight colored paper clips for each child

▷ A pencil for each child

▷ Paper and crayons for each child (for the Follow-up Activity)

Procedure

1. Distribute a tagboard strip, eight paper clips, and a pencil to each child. Then read the following situations. After each, have the children put a paper clip somewhere on the strip to show how a teacher might feel: happy, sad, or somewhere in between. Instruct children to write the letter corresponding to each situation (A, B, C, and so on) beside that paper clip.

   A: Elena got all of her spelling words right.

   B: Tyler finished first in the relay race.

   C: Ana Maria forgot her lunch money.

   D: Tyrone got all his math problems right.

   E: Sara had to read out loud, and she didn't know all the words.

   F: Angela got a gold star on her reading worksheet.

   G: Ethan lost his social studies assignment.

   H: Demetrius was the first one to finish the test.

2. Review the following by having children raise their hands and look around to see how others respond.

   ▶ Did you have all the paper clips beside the happy face? If so, raise your hands.

   ▶ Did you have all the paper clips beside the sad face? If so, raise your hands.

   ▶ Did anyone have some of the paper clips in between the sad and happy faces? If so, raise your hands.

   ▶ Which letters did you have beside the happy face?

   To make this more concrete for the children, draw a continuum on the chalkboard and write the "happy face" letters down as they recite them.

3. Next follow the same procedure for the "sad face" situations.

   ▶ Which letters did you have beside the sad face?

   ▶ Can you think of anything worse than these situations–that would have made the teacher very unhappy?

4. Share the following, then discuss the Content and Personalization Questions:

   Elena got all of her spelling words right, and you think that the teacher would be happy about this. Suppose that tomorrow, Elena misses some words. Would this make her teacher unhappy? Would it mean that the teacher doesn't like Elena because she missed some words? Sometimes we think this . . . that someone will disapprove of us, or not like us, if we make mistakes or do something wrong. But this isn't true. Your teacher won't like you any less because you do something wrong. He or she may try to help you do better, but that doesn't mean the teacher doesn't like you because you made a mistake. Sometimes kids your age get stomachaches or don't want to go to school because they are afraid they won't please their teacher. What you need to remember is that teachers are in school to help you. Sometimes they don't like it when you forget things or if you hurt someone or break a rule. But that doesn't mean that they don't like you. It just means you need to try harder to follow the rules and do the best you can with your work.

Discussion

CONTENT QUESTIONS

1. If you make a mistake or forget something or do something wrong, does this mean your teacher won't like you? What does it mean?

2. Are there some things that teachers would be more unhappy about than other things? (Ask children to share examples.)

1. Have you ever thought that your teacher didn't like you because you did something wrong?
2. What do you need to tell yourself the next time you make a mistake or do something that you think your teacher will disapprove of? Think about the example with Elena to help you answer.

Follow-up Activity

Have children divide a sheet of paper in half. On one half ask them to draw a picture to illustrate breaking a rule, making a mistake, or getting something wrong on an assignment. On the other half, have them draw a picture to show how a teacher might handle this. They can put these pages inside their desks to remind themselves that while they should try to do their best, their teacher won't dislike them if they make mistakes.

Feeling Fine, a Little Fine, or Not So Fine

Developmental Perspective

Given their concrete thinking patterns, children this age often see their feelings as being at either end of a continuum: fine or not fine, happy or unhappy, mad or glad. Helping them begin to differentiate degrees of feeling enables children to more accurately identify how they are feeling as well as to understand that there are many different ways of feeling.

Objective

▷ To learn to differentiate degrees of emotion

Materials

▷ One egg carton for each child (have children bring these from home)
▷ Twelve blank slips of paper (in an envelope) and a pencil for each child

Procedure

1. Introduce the activity by distributing the egg cartons and the envelopes containing the slips of paper.

2. Ask each child to take out four slips of paper from the envelope and write the words *elated, very unhappy, furious,* and *upset.* Have them place the first two words (*elated* and *very unhappy*) at opposite ends of one row of the egg carton and the other two words (*furious* and *upset*) at opposite ends on the other row of the egg carton.

3. As a group, discuss the concept of feeling *elated* (or very, very happy). Ask each child to think of a time she or he has felt that way. Allow some time for sharing. Then discuss the concept of feeling *very unhappy* in contrast to feeling elated. Invite sharing of times children have felt very unhappy as opposed to elated. Then discuss the fact that we can't feel just elated or very unhappy about an event–that there will be times when we feel "in between." Work with children to describe those in-between feelings: *elated, very happy, happy, a little happy, a little unhappy, very unhappy,* and so forth. Have them write these words on the slips of paper and place them where they belong in the egg-carton continuum.

4. Follow this same procedure with the words *furious* and *upset.* After children have discussed times when they have felt furious and upset, work with them to identify the "in-between" words.

5. Next ask children to identify a time when they felt one of the feelings identified in any of the in-between slots on the *furious* to *upset* continuum. Invite children to share the event associated with the feeling, then ask if they originally had felt *furious* and then later felt something further along the continuum. See if they can verbalize how that feeling changed from intense to less intense. Do the same for the *elated* to *very unhappy* continuum.

6. Process the activity by asking the Content and Personalization Questions.

Discussion

CONTENT QUESTIONS

1. Were you surprised to see several different words between the two extremes?
2. Was it difficult for you to think of words to describe these "in-between" feelings?
3. What new words did you add to your feelings vocabulary today?

PERSONALIZATION QUESTIONS

1. Do you usually experience the feelings at one end or the other on the continuum, or somewhere in between?
2. Are you usually able to recognize that you don't just feel sad or glad, but that there are lots of different points in between?
3. What did you learn in this activity that might be helpful to you in identifying your feelings?

Follow-up Activity

Ask children to identify a new set of words to put at the opposite ends of the continuum and encourage them to figure out the in-between feelings.

Boys Do, Girls Do

Developmental Perspective

Children in middle childhood gradually develop more rigid friendship patterns and tend to choose friends of the same gender. Not only does this have a limiting effect on their choice of friends, it also reinforces stereotypical thinking, which may negatively affect relationships as children get older.

Objectives

▷ To identify examples of stereotypes

▷ To learn that stereotypes do not dictate what boys and girls can and cannot do

Materials

▷ Chalkboard

▷ Two large manila envelopes, one labeled *boys* and one labeled *girls*

▷ Magazines, scissors, two sheets of paper, and crayons for each child

▷ A roll of masking tape

▷ Two pieces of newsprint. On one, write *I do.* On the other, write *I don't.*

▷ A newsprint version of the Boys Do, Girls Do–Chart (Handout 3)

▷ A long sheet of butcher paper (for the Follow-up Activity)

▷ Magazines, scissors, and glue for each child (for the Follow-up Activity)

Procedure

1. Introduce the activity by distributing the magazines, scissors, paper, and crayons. Instruct children to look through the magazines and find two pictures of things they like to do and cut them out. If they can't find pictures, they can use the paper and crayons to draw their pictures.

2. After everyone has found or drawn two examples, pass around the envelope labeled *girls* and ask only the girls to put their pictures inside. Then pass around the envelope labeled *boys,* asking only the boys to put their pictures inside.

3. Next invite children to sit in a circle around you. Open the first envelope and ask a volunteer to take out the pictures, one at a time, and describe what is being shown. Write these situations on the chalkboard under the heading *girls.* Do the same for the boys' envelope under the heading *boys.*

4. After all the pictures have been shared, look at the lists. Draw a circle around all of the items that appear on both lists. Then discuss Content Questions 1 and 2.

5. Next, post the *I do* sign in one corner of the room and the *I don't* sign in another corner. Then hang the newsprint version of the Boys Do, Girls Do–Chart (Handout 3) so that everyone can see it. Indicate to children that you will be reading some items from the chart. As you read the first item, children should (without speaking) move to either the *I do* or the *I don't* corner of the room. Before reading the next item, record on the chart the number of boys and the number of girls who are standing in each corner. Continue with this procedure until all items have been read and recorded. Then discuss Content Questions 3 and 4.

6. Discuss the remaining Content Question and the Personalization Questions.

Discussion

CONTENT QUESTIONS

1. Were there any items on both lists?

2. How many of the items were different?

3. Were there both boys and girls who could do most of the items on the chart?

4. Were there any items that none of the boys could do? Were there any items that none of the girls could do?

5. Do you ever hear kids saying that "boys can't do that" or "girls can't do that"? Do you think this is true–that there are certain things you can't do because you are a boy or that you can't do because you are a girl? (Invite sharing of examples. Try to help children think of exceptions by asking members of the opposite sex if they ever do what is being discussed or know anyone of their gender who does.)

PERSONALIZATION QUESTIONS

1. Do you ever think there are certain things you can't do because you are a boy or a girl? If so, how do you feel about this?

2. Do you think it is actually true that you can't do certain things, or do you just think you can't because you have seen advertisements showing only boys or only girls doing them, or because someone has told you that only boys or only girls do them?

3. What did you learn from this lesson?

Follow-up Activity

Take a long sheet of butcher paper and hang it in the room. Label it *boys and girls do*. Invite children to cut out or draw pictures of things they do and glue these pictures on the butcher paper to form a collage.

Boys Do, Girls Do

CHART

	Boys do	Girls do
Run fast		
Climb a tree		
Jump rope		
Swim		
Use imagination		
Spell words		
Ride a bike		
Rollerblade		
Play school		
Play house		

Together Is Better

Developmental Perspective

Middle childhood signifies the acquisition of many new skills. Learning to work well with others is one skill important for children's cognitive as well as social development. Through work with others they learn "give and take" skills, the art of compromise, and the satisfaction that comes from contributing to team goals.

Objectives

▷ To distinguish between cooperative and uncooperative behaviors

▷ To practice cooperative behaviors

Materials

▷ Several large sheets of butcher paper (or newspapers)

▷ Two rolls of masking tape (one per group)

▷ A copy of the Together Is Better–Team Instructions (Handout 4) for Team 1 and Team 2

▷ A Together Is Better–Observer Sheet (Handout 5) and a pencil for each child who is not on a team

▷ A video camera (optional)

▷ A newsprint version of the Together Is Better–Observer Sheet (for the Follow-up Activity)

Procedure

1. Introduce the lesson by explaining that two teams will demonstrate two different ways to work on a project. Children should watch closely and be ready to discuss the differences in the way these two teams work.

2. Select two teams of five children each. Give the first team the Together Is Better–Team Instructions for Team 1 (Handout 4) and briefly review them so others in the room cannot hear. Do the same with the instructions for Team 2.

3. Emphasize that those who are not on a team have an important role as observers. Give a Together Is Better–Observer Sheet (Handout 5) to each child who is not on a team. Review the sheet so observers understand how to respond.

4. Ask Team 1 to do their project first. Allow approximately 15 minutes. When they have finished, ask the observers to share their observations. Elicit specific examples of positive and negative behaviors, and discuss how these behaviors affected the outcome. Ask team members how they felt about their final product and their participation on the team.

5. Ask Team 2 to do their project. Follow the same procedure, with observers sharing their reports after approximately 15 minutes. (This group will not complete the task.)

Leader note: If a video camera is available, teams could be videotaped as they work and the video played back so children can see examples of cooperative and uncooperative behavior.

6. Process the activity by asking the Content and Personalization Questions.

Discussion

CONTENT QUESTIONS

1. What kinds of behaviors do you need to demonstrate to work cooperatively as a team member?

2. If you were uncooperative, what behaviors would you demonstrate?

3. When you work with others, do you think it is important to cooperate? Why or why not?

4. What are some of the reasons people don't cooperate?

PERSONALIZATION QUESTIONS

1. What is the most difficult thing for you about cooperating and working as a good team member?

2. In what ways are you good at cooperating and team-member behaviors?

3. If you aren't a very good team member, what behaviors would help you improve?

Follow-up Activity

Post the newsprint version of the Together Is Better–Observer Sheet. As children work in groups on science, math, or social studies projects, have them refer to it to help them identify cooperative versus uncooperative behaviors.

Together Is Better

TEAM INSTRUCTIONS

Leader note: Make one copy and cut apart; give one set of instructions to each team.

TEAM 1

Choose a leader for the group by a show of hands. The leader should clearly state the problem: to build a short tunnel out of paper and masking tape, large enough for team members to crawl through one at a time. Everyone in the group should share ideas about how to build the tunnel before the team begins to work. The leader will select the specific idea out of those suggested, and the team will begin to work after the leader has assigned a job to everyone. Members will work cooperatively until they finish the tunnel.

TEAM 2

Everyone yells out at once to be the leader. Argue about that for a minute, then decide that you don't really need a leader. Then have one person read the task: to build a short tunnel out of paper and masking tape, large enough for all team members to crawl through one at a time. Everyone in the group should start shouting out ideas. No one listens to anyone. Finally, one person should say that the group should try his or her idea. The others agree, but they do not finish the tunnel because they don't cooperate (they don't share the tape, they tell others that the ideas are dumb, and so forth).

Together Is Better

OBSERVER SHEET

Name: _____ Date: _____

Instructions: Watch the way each team works. Put an X beside each behavior you see the team members doing.

	Team 1	Team 2
Share ideas		
Cooperate		
Yell		
Argue		
Share supplies		
Agree with others		
Listen to others		
Finish the job		

Find a Friend

Developmental Perspective

Socialization in the context of a peer group is a central issue during middle childhood. Acceptance and "best friend" issues consume a good deal of children's energy. Because conflicts and negative feelings are often related to friendship situations, enhancing skills in making and keeping friends is important at this stage of social development.

Objectives

▷ To enhance skills in making and keeping friends
▷ To practice friendship behaviors

Materials

▷ Chalkboard
▷ A set of Find a Friend–Statements and Responses (Handout 6)

Procedure

1. Ask children to think about a good friend and something this friend does that they think is an example of a good friendship skill. Invite children to share ideas without stating names.

2. Next randomly distribute the Find a Friend–Statements and Responses (Handout 6), one to each child. Explain that children are to *silently* walk around the room and show their slips of paper to one another. When they think they have found a person whose slip matches theirs, they should find a spot to sit down together and talk about how to be a good friend. When all children have had a chance to discuss briefly, invite sharing of ideas with the total group and list ideas on the chalkboard.

3. To process the activity, discuss the Content and Personalization Questions.

Discussion

CONTENT QUESTIONS

1. Did you have a difficult time finding your partner?
2. Do you think most children practice positive friendship skills? If not, do you think children would get along better if they did?

PERSONALIZATION QUESTIONS

1. Do you think your friendship skills are positive or negative?

2. What ideas did you and your partner or others in the group identify that you think you will practice in order to make or keep friends?

Follow-up Activity

Invite children to identify two friendship behaviors they will practice during the week and write these on the back of their friendship slips. Provide time for them to report back on how this practice affected their relationships with others.

Find a Friend

STATEMENTS AND RESPONSES

Leader note: Cut statements and responses into separate slips; give each child one slip.

Statements	Responses
I like your jacket.	Thank you.
Do you want to play kickball?	Sure–thanks for asking me.
I liked your ideas for the group project.	I liked your ideas, too.
Can you come to my birthday party?	Yes–thanks for inviting me.
I had fun at your house yesterday.	I had fun, too.
Do you want some of my crackers?	No, thanks.
She's sitting all alone. Let's ask her to sit with us.	That's a good idea.
We played what I wanted to yesterday, so it's your turn to choose today.	I like taking turns.
I've got a secret to tell you.	I won't tell anyone.
I'm sorry you couldn't come to my party.	Me too–but I'm glad you asked me.
I'm glad you won the class president election.	Thanks for telling me.
You're fun to play with.	I like playing with you, too.

They Didn't Choose Me

Developmental Perspective

As children expand their social networks, the risk of rejection increases. For many children, rejection can be very difficult. However, since rejection is a common phenomenon that children will continue to experience in various ways throughout childhood and adolescence, they must learn healthy ways to deal with it.

Objectives

▷ To identify ways to deal with rejection

▷ To recognize that one is not worthless if rejected by others

Materials

▷ Chalkboard

▷ A pair of equally desirable (but different) age-appropriate toys

▷ Several advertisements for (or actual boxes of) different kinds of cereal

▷ A copy of the They Didn't Choose Me–Story (Handout 7). This can be read to the children or they can each have a copy to read, depending on ability.

Procedure

1. Display the pair of objects and encourage a discussion about which toy children prefer. Emphasize the fact that children make different choices based on their preferences, but that does not mean there is something wrong with the toy some children didn't select. Extend this to include how children select friends: Is there something wrong with someone just because some people don't select him or her as a friend?

2. Elicit and list on the chalkboard situations in which children are chosen: as a study partner, as a team member, as a best friend, or as someone to invite to a party, for example. Discuss why children make the selections they do: For example, in selecting a study partner, they would want someone who knows a lot about the subject and is a hard worker. In selecting a best friend, they would probably want someone who doesn't tell their secrets, someone they like to play with, and so on. Stress the fact that we choose people for different reasons.

3. Present the cereal advertisements or boxes one at a time. Have children raise a hand if that cereal is their very favorite–the one they would choose ahead of all others. As you present each cereal, ask a child to record the name of the cereal and the number of children who indicated that this was their favorite on the chalkboard. After all the cereals have been presented, review the findings. Engage

children in a brief discussion about the fact that everyone has different reasons for selecting something. Ask them if the other cereals are no good just because some people didn't select them. Indicate that this is the same for people: If someone doesn't select them for something, it doesn't mean they are worthless or no good.

4. Invite children to read or listen to the They Didn't Choose Me–Story (Handout 7). Follow with the Content and Personalization Questions.

Discussion

CONTENT QUESTIONS

1. How was Elena *feeling* about not being selected as a group leader and being chosen last for the group?

2. What was Elena *thinking* about not being selected as a group leader and being chosen last for the group?

3. Do you believe what Elena was thinking was true (that nobody liked her, that she had dumb ideas, and so on)?

4. Do you think others your age experience the same kinds of thoughts and feelings that Elena did if they are chosen last or not selected for something?

5. What did Carmen say that helped Elena feel somewhat better about the situation?

PERSONALIZATION QUESTIONS

1. Have you ever experienced what Elena did?

2. If you have been chosen last or not chosen at all, have you had some of the same kinds of thoughts and feelings as Elena? (Invite sharing.)

3. If you have been chosen last or not chosen at all, how have you handled it?

4. What can you think to yourself to help you deal with not being chosen if this happens to you again?

Follow-up Activity

Invite children to interview parents or older siblings to see if they have ever experienced rejection. Have the children ask questions such as the following:

- ► Have you ever been rejected or chosen last for something?
- ► How did you feel when this happened?
- ► Did you think nobody liked you or you were no good? Were these things really true?
- ► How did you handle this?

Have children write a short report or story about their interview to share with the group.

They Didn't Choose Me

STORY–PAGE 1

Elena was eager for school to get out so she could go home and tell her family some good news! Today her teacher, Mr. Herrera, had informed the class that they were going to be working on projects to raise money so they could take a field trip to the zoo and the natural history museum. Elena was really excited because she had only been to the zoo once, and she had been too little to remember much about it. She had never been to a museum, and her teacher had said that this one was one of the neatest because it had a huge dinosaur exhibit and lots of other interesting things.

At school the next day, Mr. Herrera explained more about their projects. He said that they would first be working in groups to think of ways to earn enough money to pay for the bus ride, their entrance fees to the zoo and the museum, and lunch and snacks. After the groups came up with ideas, the entire class would select five that looked like the best ways to raise the most money. Mr. Herrera told the class that they would be working in groups after lunch recess.

At lunch that day, Elena sat with Juanita. She and Juanita weren't best friends, but they sometimes sat beside each other at lunch. Today they were both excited about the field trip and the class projects. Throughout lunch they talked about their ideas.

When they got back to the classroom after lunch recess, Mr. Herrera selected four students to be the group leaders: Juanita, Peter, Ramon, and Chelsea. Elena was really upset. She had wanted to be a leader. She wondered why Mr. Herrera hadn't chosen her: Didn't he like her? Did he think she wasn't smart enough to be a good leader? Was it because she wasn't as popular as the students he chose? All of these thoughts kept rumbling through her mind. It bothered her that she hadn't been selected; she couldn't understand what was wrong with her. *(Stop and ask the children why they think Elena wasn't selected. List their ideas on the chalkboard.)*

They Didn't Choose Me

STORY–PAGE 2

Then the group leaders started choosing teams. Elena kept her fingers crossed that Juanita would pick her, but Juanita first chose Kelly. "Why didn't she choose me?" Elena wondered. "She knows I have some ideas because we were talking about it at lunch. Did she think they were dumb? Did I do something that made her mad?" Elena was confused and getting unhappier by the minute. *(Stop and ask children why they think Juanita didn't pick Elena.)*

As the other group leaders started choosing their members, Elena became increasingly nervous. Ramon chose Tony, Peter chose Serita, and Chelsea chose Carmen. Then it was Juanita's turn to choose again. Elena held her breath, hoping she would be the next one Juanita selected. But then she heard Juanita call out Carlos's name. Elena blinked back the tears and listened as the other leaders each chose another person. No one was calling her name. Elena felt like running out of the room. It was so embarrassing to still be sitting there when others were joining the groups. Elena wanted to crawl in a hole.

Finally, there were three students left: Elena, Jonathan, and Mark. It was Chelsea's turn to choose. She called Mark's name. Then it was Ramon's turn to choose. He asked Jonathan to join his group. Elena was the only one left. She felt so bad she could hardly make her feet move across the floor when Peter called her name. She knew he didn't have a choice since everyone else was already in a group, and she wished she could disappear.

But Elena didn't disappear, and she had to join the group. She kept her head down so other kids wouldn't see how close to tears she was. She pulled a chair into the group and just sat there. Mr. Herrera announced that all groups should start thinking of money-making projects and write their ideas down. Elena was quiet the whole time; she didn't feel like sharing her ideas. In fact, she didn't even care if she ever went to the zoo or the museum.

They Didn't Choose Me

STORY—PAGE 3

So as the other children got excited about their ideas, Elena sat there like a bump on a log. Finally, it was time to go home from school. Elena quietly picked up her books and walked out the door, shuffling along with her head down. She was half-way across the playground before Carmen caught up with her. "Elena, what's wrong? You didn't wait for me like you usually do," said Carmen.

"I just figured you wouldn't want to walk home with me," said Elena.

"Why's that?" asked Carmen.

"Well, why would you want to walk home with me since no one else wants to be with me," said Elena.

"What do you mean?" asked Carmen.

"You know what I mean. I was the last one chosen to be on a team. Nobody wanted to work with me. There must be something wrong with me. Even Mr. Herrera doesn't like me because he didn't pick me to be a team leader. I hate the whole idea of these group projects. I don't even want to go on the field trip."

"Elena, just because you got chosen last doesn't mean nobody likes you. Sometimes that's just the way it is. Yesterday I was just about the last one chosen for the game during gym class. I didn't like it, but somebody has to be last. So today I was one of the first. That's just the way it goes sometimes. I think you got picked yesterday before I did, didn't you?"

Elena slowly shook her head. "Yeah, I guess I did. But today was a lot more important. I just felt so dumb sitting there when everyone else was joining a group."

"I know," said Carmen. "I've felt like that, too. But do you really think nobody likes you just because you were the last one to get chosen today? How can that be true if I'm walking home with you and if Juanita sat with you at lunch? Sure, you were the last one picked today, but that doesn't mean you'll always be the last, does it?"

They Didn't Choose Me

STORY–PAGE 4

"Well, maybe not," said Elena. "I just felt so weird sitting there practically all by myself. It made me feel like I had bad germs or something."

"Well, you don't have germs, and you can't just go on thinking that you'll always get chosen last because then you'll be sad all the time and nobody will want to play with you or have you on their team. So start thinking of your ideas and how much fun it's going to be to go on the field trip," encouraged Carmen.

The next day Elena joined her group. She remembered what she and Carmen had talked about on the way home from school, so she shared her ideas with the group. They thought Elena's ideas were really good, and Elena was hopeful that at least one of hers might be a project the whole class would do to raise money for the trip.

Big, Little, or In-Between Decisions

Developmental Perspective

As children mature, they will increasingly make decisions that will affect their lives. Because they are still concrete thinkers, children often have difficulty seeing the many different factors involved in the decision-making process and differentiating between major and minor decisions.

Objectives

▷ To begin to distinguish big, little, and in-between decisions

▷ To identify different factors to consider when making different types of decisions

Materials

▷ Two packages of gum (different kinds)

▷ A 10-dollar bill

▷ A picture of the President of the United States

▷ A copy of the Big, Little, or In-Between Decisions–Decision Ladders (Handout 8) and crayons for each partnership

▷ Another copy of the Decision Ladders and crayons for each child (for the Follow-up Activity)

Procedure

1. Introduce the lesson by showing children the two different kinds of gum. Ask children who prefer the first kind to raise a hand, then children who prefer the second kind to raise a hand. Then ask them if they think that deciding what kind of gum to chew is a *big decision,* a *little decision,* or an *in-between decision.*

2. Next hold up the 10-dollar bill. Tell children to imagine that you are giving each of them this amount of money and that they need to decide how to spend it. Ask them if they think this is a *big decision,* a *little decision,* or an *in-between decision.*

3. Then display the picture of the President of the United States. Tell children to imagine that they are the president and have to decide whether the country will go to war against another country. Again, have them evaluate this as a *big, little,* or *in-between decision.*

4. Discuss the differences among these three types of decisions. First, ask children if they think everyone is always in agreement about whether a decision is big, little, or in-between. Discuss the fact that while there are usually some decisions that most people would consider big or little, whether or not someone thinks a decision is big, little, or in-between depends on the person. Elicit other factors that distinguish these types of decisions. For example:

   ► Little decisions might not affect as many people.

   ► Little decisions are usually not as important as big decisions.

   ► Little decisions might not have as many consequences as big decisions.

   ► The consequences of little decisions are usually not as important as the consequences of big decisions.

   Emphasize the fact that some decisions may fall in between the big and the little.

5. Ask children to find a partner. Distribute a copy of the Big, Little, or In-Between Decisions–Decision Ladders (Handout 8) to each partnership. Inform children that you will be reading some decisions. As you read each one, partners are to discuss whether they would consider this a *big, little,* or *in-between decision,* write the number of the decision on the Decision Ladder that represents the choice agreed on by both (*big, little,* or *in-between*), and take turns coloring the space on the ladder that matches their choice.

BIG, LITTLE, OR IN-BETWEEN DECISIONS

► Decision 1: You are at the candy store, and you really want a candy bar. You can't decide whether you should take one when the clerk isn't looking or just leave without it.

► Decision 2: You can't decide whether to wear your Bulls sweatshirt or your Miami Heat sweatshirt to school.

► Decision 3: You are playing with a friend. You can't decide if you should play outside or inside.

► Decision 4: You are at the store with your mother. You can't decide whether you should stay with her as she told you to do or go look at the pets, which is what you want to do.

► Decision 5: In the cafeteria you can choose a hot dog or a cheese sandwich. You can't decide which one you want.

► Decision 6: Your stepmother said you can bring one friend with you when you come to spend the weekend. You can't decide which friend to invite.

► Decision 7: Your worst subject is math. The kid sitting in front of you is really good at it. You are trying to decide if you should look over his shoulder to get his answers.

► Decision 8: A friend told you a secret and you promised not to tell, but another friend is asking you about the secret. You are trying to decide if you should tell or not.

> ► Decision 9: You are supposed to go right home from school, but you want to play in the park. You have to make a decision quickly because your friends are waiting for an answer.
>
> ► Decision 10: You can't decide if you want vanilla or chocolate ice cream.

6. Process the activity by asking the Content and Personalization Questions.

Discussion

CONTENT QUESTIONS

1. Which type of decisions did you and your partner have the most of?

2. How did you decide which type of decision to choose? What things did you have to consider to make your decision?

3. What makes a decision a big decision? A little decision? An in-between decision?

PERSONALIZATION QUESTIONS

1. Have you ever had to make a big decision? What made it big for you?

2. What are some little decisions you have made?

3. When you have a big decision to make, do you usually make it alone, or do others help you?

4. Do you think you make good decisions? If not, what can you do to change that?

Follow-up Activity

Have students create a list of the big, little, and in-between decisions they make for one week. Have them color the appropriate spaces on another copy of the Decision Ladders to help them learn more about the types of decisions they generally make. Share children's decisions in a follow-up discussion.

Big, Little, or In-Between Decisions

DECISION LADDERS

BIG DECISIONS　　　　　**LITTLE DECISIONS**　　　　　**IN-BETWEEN DECISIONS**

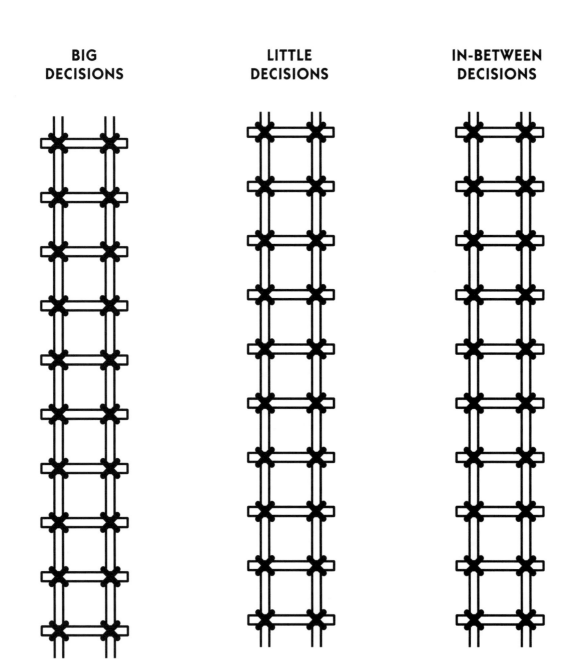

What Happens If?

Developmental Perspective

Despite the fact that many important cognitive changes are occurring at this stage of development, children this age are still guided more by their feelings than by reason. They also fail to integrate their experiences and do not see complex connections between events. It is therefore critical to teach them to anticipate consequences so they don't experience negative repercussions.

Objective

▷ To learn how to anticipate consequences

Materials

▷ Eight large word cards (one for each word: *push, fall, hunt, find, listen, learn, eat, grow*)

▷ A roll of masking tape

▷ One What Happens If? Situation (Handout 9) for each group of four children

▷ Paper and a pencil for each child (for the Follow-up Activity)

Procedure

1. Introduce the lesson by displaying the word cards one at a time in random order. As you display each word, tape it to the wall and ask children to read the word aloud. After the words have all been introduced, ask children which words could be paired because one action would logically result in another. Rearrange the words in pairs as children identify them: *push/fall, hunt/find, listen/learn, eat/grow.*

2. Discuss the concept of logical consequences: being able to anticipate what can happen based on an action. For example, if you hear thunder, you can logically predict that it will rain. Ask children for other examples, such as anticipating that the teacher will get mad if she tells children to be quiet and they keep talking. Ask children what would probably happen if you changed the initial action. For example, if you didn't keep talking, would the teacher get mad? Ask children for other examples.

3. Next divide children into groups of four. Give each group one of the What Happens If? Situations (Handout 9). Tell children that their task is to think about what would happen based on the information given and develop a short skit to act this out. (It might be good to demonstrate this process by asking several children to come to the front and listen as you read one situation. Then have them discuss who the characters in the skit should be, who would say what to whom, and how they could get their point across to others.)

4. After each group presents, reread their situation and discuss other possible logical consequences.

5. To process the activity, discuss the Content and Personalization Questions.

Discussion

CONTENT QUESTIONS

1. How did your group decide what would happen based on the information you had in your situation?

2. Do you think it is a good idea to think ahead to *what happens if?*
   If so, why do you think it would be good to do this?

PERSONALIZATION QUESTIONS

1. Can you think of a time when you were able to think ahead to what might happen if you did something? Did this change your behavior in any way?

2. Have you ever forgotten to think ahead? If so, what happened when you didn't?

3. What did you learn from this lesson that might help you in future situations?

Follow-up Activity

Invite children to write two short stories: one about a character who doesn't think ahead and what happens to him or her, and the other about a character who does think ahead and what the outcome is. Provide time for children to share their stories.

What Happens If?

SITUATIONS

Leader note: Cut situations apart; give each group of four children one situation.

SITUATION 1

You are standing outside the door at school and a stranger comes up to you. He says he works with your mom and she had to work overtime, so she asked him to pick you up and take you home. If you go with him, what could happen?

SITUATION 2

Your church group is planning to sleep in tents in back of the church. You are afraid to stay outside in a tent, but you don't want to tell your friends that you are afraid. What could happen if you do?

SITUATION 3

Your parents had to work late. They called and told you to stay in the house and not have anyone over. One of your friends calls and asks to come over to play. If you say yes, what could happen?

SITUATION 4

You are supposed to be home for supper at 6:00, but you are right in the middle of a great kickball game. What could happen if you stay long enough to finish the game (another 15 minutes)?

SITUATION 5

Your dad says you have to clean your room before you go to the movies. You have been watching television, and time is running out. What happens if you just stuff everything under your bed and tell him you're done cleaning?

SITUATION 6

You really want to buy a new Power Ranger, but you don't have quite enough money. When you were in your brother's room, you noticed some money on the dresser. What would happen if you took it?

Solve It

Developmental Perspective

At this stage of development, children are more capable of gathering and organizing facts and can look at things more logically. They are able to solve more challenging problems and use strategies for remembering. Reinforcing these skills can enhance their cognitive development.

Objective

▷ To recognize and use problem-solving strategies

Materials

▷ Chalkboard

▷ Enough magazine pictures of a food item or toy for half the children in the group

▷ A roll of masking tape

▷ A newsprint version of the Solve It–Problem-Solving Steps (Handout 10)

▷ One Solve It–Dilemma (Handout 11) for each group of three children

▷ A copy of the Solve It–Problem-Solving Steps for each child (for the Follow-up Activity)

Procedure

1. Begin the lesson by dividing the group in half. Take one of these groups and tape a magazine picture to each child's back. (Children are not to see the pictures.) Then have each child who doesn't have a picture find one who does. Instruct pairs to find a place in the room to sit down. Caution the child without the picture not to tell his or her partner what the picture is. Explain that the children who have pictures must find out what their pictures are by asking their partners questions. Indicate that the pictures are either of a toy or something to eat. Children with pictures should phrase their questions in such a way that their partners can give them "clues." For example, instead of asking, "Is it a toy gun?" they should ask a broader question, such as "Would this be a toy that you would usually play with outside or inside?"

2. Allow some time for children to try to guess their pictures, then pull the group together to discuss what strategies they used in trying to solve this problem.

3. Present the newsprint version of the Solve It–Problem-Solving Steps (Handout 10). Introduce these steps and point out that they are written in the form of questions to ask when solving a problem. Discuss the steps in relation to the problem children just solved, as suggested by the italicized questions and comments.

> ► Step 1: What is the problem?
> *The problem is to find out what the picture is.*

> ► Step 2: What information do you need?
> *Gather clues: For example, ask, "Do you play with it inside or outside?"*

> ► Step 3: What are possible solutions?
> *Is it a toy that both boys and girls like to play with?*

> ► Step 4: What might be the consequences of each of these solutions?
> *None in this simulation; use another example to illustrate the concept.*

> ► Step 5: Which solutions will you eliminate?
> *For example, ask yourself, "If it is not a toy to play with outside, then it must be (a toy to play with inside)."*

> ► Step 6: Which solution will you choose?
> *Arrive at a solution after eliminating options. (Have children state what their pictures were.)*

4. Divide children into groups of three and distribute a Solve It–Dilemma to each group (see Handout 11). (Several groups may have the same dilemma.) Have them refer to the problem-solving steps, as written on the sheet of newsprint, and use the problem-solving process to arrive at a solution.

5. Allow time for groups to share their solutions and review the steps in the problem-solving process, then discuss the Content and Personalization Questions.

Discussion

CONTENT QUESTIONS

1. How did the problem-solving process work for your group?

2. Which step is the most difficult? Which is the easiest?

3. Which step do you think is the most important?

PERSONALIZATION QUESTIONS

1. When you try to solve a problem, do you use a process like this? If not, how do you arrive at a solution?

2. When you have a problem to solve, do you usually consider lots of solutions or just a few? Which do you think is best?

3. When you solve a problem, how do you usually feel about your solutions?

Follow-up Activity

Give children a copy of the Solve It–Problem-Solving Steps to take home. Ask them to interview parents or older siblings about how they use this process to solve their problems. Provide time for children to share the results of their interviews. Keep the newsprint version of the problem-solving steps posted in the room so children can refer to it when they have a problem to solve.

Solve It

PROBLEM-SOLVING STEPS

STEP 1   What is the problem?

STEP 2   What information do you need?

STEP 3   What are possible solutions?

STEP 4   What might be the consequences
of each of these solutions?

STEP 5   Which solutions will you eliminate?

STEP 6   Which solution will you choose?

Solve It

DILEMMAS

Leader note: Cut dilemmas apart; give each group of three children one dilemma.

DILEMMA 1

You are a patrol guard at the school crosswalk. Every night after school some older kids come by and tease you and threaten you. You think if you tell the principal, the older kids might find out.

DILEMMA 2

You are taking a test. You see the person next to you looking over at someone else's paper. You think it is wrong to cheat, and you don't think this kid should get by with it.

DILEMMA 3

Your dad and stepmother invite you to go on a trip with them, but it is at the same time your mom was planning to take you to an amusement park.

DILEMMA 4

Your grandparents gave you a new bike for your birthday. Your parents warned you about leaving it in the yard, but you were in a hurry and left it outside overnight. When you came out this morning, your bike was gone. Your grandparents are coming over tonight to see you ride the new bike.

Thinking Makes It So

Developmental Perspective

Despite the number of cognitive changes throughout middle childhood, children at this age are still guided more by feelings than by reason. This affects their decision-making process as well as their behavior. Increasing their capacity to reason and make rational decisions is an important aspect of their development.

Objectives

▷ To identify how thinking influences feelings and actions

▷ To identify the negative consequences of acting on thoughts without checking them out

Materials

▷ None

Procedure

1. Introduce the lesson by asking children to close their eyes and imagine they are going to move to a big city in another part of the country. Ask all children who would be excited about the thought of moving to stand up, keeping their eyes closed. Then ask the children who wouldn't want to move to raise a hand. Have children open their eyes and count the number who are standing and the number who have a hand raised. Engage children in a discussion about why they felt differently about the same event. For example, the children who are excited might see this as an adventure, or they might not like living where they do. The children who don't want to move might not want to leave their neighborhood, their friends, and so on.

2. Emphasize the fact that how we *think* about something affects the way we *feel* about it, as illustrated in the example. How we *think* also affects what we *do* about something. To demonstrate, ask two volunteers to come to the front of the group. In private, direct one volunteer to stomp his or her feet on the floor and throw a fit in response to the situation you present. The other volunteer is only going to look disappointed or sad. Then explain to the group that these two volunteers are going to take turns reacting to what you say to them. Turn to the volunteers and say, "You won't be able to go to the skating party because you didn't pick up your room and feed your pets like you were supposed to do." Point to Volunteer 1, who throws a fit, and then to Volunteer 2, who just looks sad and disappointed. Discuss with the children the differences in the way Volunteers 1 and 2 behaved. Elicit from them why they think these two volunteers behaved differently: What must the first volunteer have been thinking to make him or her angry enough to throw a fit? What must the second volunteer have been thinking to act just sad or disappointed? Emphasize the connection between thoughts and actions.

3. Next invite children to listen as you read the following story, about how a third grader's thoughts influenced her actions. After reading the story, discuss the Content and Personalization Questions.

THINKING MAKES IT SO–STORY

It was Monday morning. Jenny had been up late the night before because her parents were yelling and screaming at each other, and she couldn't get to sleep. She was lost in her own thoughts when she got on the bus, and she took the first seat she saw. She didn't even notice her friend Dawn sitting two seats behind her. But Dawn noticed Jenny and immediately became upset because Jenny didn't sit by her; they always sat together on the bus. Dawn thought Jenny was mad at her and didn't want to be her friend anymore.

After they got to school, Jenny just got off the bus and didn't wait for Dawn. She went straight to the classroom and sat down at her desk. Later in the morning, the teacher asked them to find a partner to work with in math. Usually Dawn and Jenny worked together, but today Dawn picked another partner because Jenny hadn't sat with her.

Jenny thought it was strange that Dawn didn't ask to be her partner, but she was still feeling upset about her parents' fight, so she didn't think about it very much. When lunch time came, Jenny's stomach hurt, and she didn't feel like talking, so she sat in a corner by herself. Dawn noticed Jenny sitting there, but she joined another group of girls. Pretty soon they were laughing and pointing at Jenny. Jenny saw them making fun of her, but she just ignored them.

After lunch the teacher told the class that they were going to work on their science projects and that she was going to assign the partners. He put Dawn and Jenny together. Jenny took out her book and walked back to where Dawn was sitting. Dawn refused to look at Jenny and completely ignored her. Jenny was getting frustrated because they had to communicate in order to finish the project. She didn't know what to do. She asked Dawn some questions about how they should do their first task, and Dawn snapped, "I don't want to work with you. Figure it out yourself." Jenny was close to tears. She didn't know why Dawn was acting this way, and now was the time she really needed a friend since things were so bad at home. She finally decided to ask the teacher if she could go to the nurse's office for the rest of the afternoon.

When it came time to get on the bus at the end of the day, Dawn saw Jenny sitting in their usual spot and deliberately chose another place to sit. They didn't talk when they got off the bus, and the next morning things were no different; Dawn still ignored her. But they had to work together again on their project, and by this time Jenny couldn't take it anymore.

"Dawn, why are you treating me this way? What did I do?"

"You didn't sit by me on the bus yesterday, that's what," said Dawn.

"The reason I didn't sit by you is because I didn't see where you were, and I just didn't feel like sitting by anyone. I was really upset because my parents yelled and screamed at each other all night, and I'm afraid they are going to get a divorce. It didn't have anything to do with you."

"Oh," said Dawn. "I'm really sorry. I just figured you didn't want to be my friend, and that made me mad."

"Well, that's not true," said Jenny. "I just had too many things to worry about. I wish you just would have asked me what was wrong and we wouldn't have had all this trouble."

"I'm sorry. I guess I should have checked it out before I started acting like that."

Discussion

CONTENT QUESTIONS

1. How did Dawn's thoughts affect her actions?
2. What do you think would have happened if Dawn hadn't assumed Jenny didn't want to be her friend because Jenny didn't sit with her? How would that have changed the whole story?
3. What could Dawn have done so she wouldn't have acted the way she did toward Jenny?

PERSONALIZATION QUESTIONS

1. Have you ever had thoughts like Dawn's, which influenced your actions? If so, what happened?
2. What do you think you will remember from this lesson that may help you make better decisions about how you act?

Follow-up Activity

Have children make up short skits to illustrate how thoughts can influence actions. Allow time for them to present these to the group. Emphasize the important connection between thoughts and actions.

the **PASSPORT** PROGRAM

Self-Development
ACTIVITY
1 Just a Mistake
2 All about Me
3 Stamp of Approval
4 I Am Someone Who . . .

Emotional Development
ACTIVITY
1 Tease Tolerance
2 War on Worries
3 I Can't Do It
4 Solutions for Sad Feelings

Social Development
ACTIVITY
1 Together We Can
2 Don't Bully Me
3 Pointers for Put-Downs
4 Rules for Relationships

Cognitive Development
ACTIVITY
1 Tunnel Vision
2 Long and Short of It
3 Really Rational
4 Problems and Solutions

Just a Mistake

Developmental Perspective

At this stage of development, children compare their skills and achievements to those of others. Their sense of competition heightens. They are often quick to put themselves down or assume that they should never make mistakes. It is important for children to realize that they cannot be perfect and they will make mistakes, but that this does not detract from their self-worth.

Objectives

▷ To learn that making mistakes is natural

▷ To learn that making mistakes does not make one a bad person

Materials

▷ A glass, a pitcher of water, and a sweater or jacket with five or more buttons

▷ One Just a Mistake–Cue Card (Handout 1) for each group of three

▷ Paper and pencil for each child (for the Follow-up Activity)

Procedure

1. Introduce the lesson by pouring water into a glass. Look away and "accidentally" miss the glass while you are pouring so water spills on the table. Elicit discussion about what happened, introducing the word *accidentally*. Ask children for examples of things they have done accidentally.

2. Next take the jacket or sweater. Ask a child to time you to see how fast you can button the buttons. Because you are in a hurry, make sure to miss one or get the buttons crooked. When you have finished, ask children how well you did and discuss the *mistake* you made by missing the button or getting the buttons crooked. Ask children for a definition of the word *mistake* (a wrong action or an error). Encourage discussion about why people make mistakes: for example, because they are in a hurry, misunderstand directions, don't recheck what they have done, accidentally forget something, or aren't sure what to do.

3. Divide children into groups of three and distribute the Just a Mistake–Cue Cards (Handout 1), one to each group. Ask children to read their cards and develop a short skit based on the information.

4. After adequate planning time, have groups present the skits.

5. To process the activity, discuss the Content and Personalization Questions.

Discussion

Content Questions

1. What mistakes were made in these skits?
2. Were any of the mistakes ones you would consider to be serious mistakes?
3. Were the children who made the mistakes "bad" because they made mistakes?
4. Do you think it is possible to learn from mistakes? If so, how?
5. Do you think you should keep on making the same mistakes over and over?
6. Do you think everyone makes mistakes sometimes?

Personalization Questions

1. Do you ever make mistakes? (Invite children to share examples.)
2. When you make a mistake, how do you feel? Do you put yourself down for making the mistake?
3. Do you think you or anyone else can be perfect and never make mistakes?
4. What can you tell yourself the next time you make a mistake so you don't get "down" on yourself or think you are a bad person because you did this?

Follow-up Activity

Ask children to imagine that someone they really care about has made a mistake. Have them write a letter to that person explaining that everyone makes mistakes, that the person can learn from the mistake, and what the person can tell himself or herself to avoid getting down about making the mistake.

Just a Mistake

CUE CARDS—PAGE 1

Leader note: Cut apart; give each group of three one cue card.

CUE CARD 1

Jane wants her friend Joanne to call her at her grandmother's house. Since Joanne doesn't know the number, she asks Jane to write it down. When Joanne gets home and tries to call the number, she doesn't get the grandmother . . . she gets a gruff-sounding man who is not Jane's grandfather. Joanne figures she made a mistake in dialing, so she tries the number again. The same person answers. Since Joanne doesn't know the grandmother's last name, she can't look up the number, so she just gives up. The next day at school Joanne sees Jane and explains what happened. Jane looks at the number she had written down and realizes she made a mistake by switching two numbers around.

Role-players: Jane, Joanne, and the gruff-sounding man

CUE CARD 2

Todd's dad tells him to be sure to feed the cat as soon as he comes home from school. However, when Todd gets home, the phone is ringing and it is his friend Ryan, who asks Todd to meet him at their tree house. Todd quickly changes his clothes and rushes outside, forgetting about the cat. When Todd's dad asks him later if Tomcat was fed, Todd has to tell him that he forgot.

Role-players: Todd, Ryan, and the dad

Just a Mistake

CUE CARDS—PAGE 2

CUE CARD 3

Sheniqua's mother says she can invite five girls to her sleepover party. Sheniqua has a hard time deciding whom to invite, but she finally makes her choices and sends out the invitations. Several days later her best friend Shantel refuses to play with her. Sheniqua asks her why, and Shantel says that it's because she wasn't invited to Sheniqua's party. Sheniqua is confused because she knows she sent Shantel an invitation. All she can think of is that the invitation was lost in the mail. When she gets home that night she tells her mother, and they look around to see if the invitation was misplaced in the house. They can't find it. The next day Shantel tells her that the invitation just arrived but it came late because Sheniqua had sent it to the wrong address.

Role-players: Sheniqua, Shantel, and the mother

Just a Mistake

CUE CARDS—PAGE 3

CUE CARD 4

Adam has a spelling test tomorrow, so he asks his older brother, Sam, to help him with the words. Sam agrees to read the words to Adam, and the first time Adam gets all but one right. Sam helps Adam practice that word, and they try again. This time Adam gets them all right. The next morning before he leaves for school Adam's mother goes over the list with him again, and he spells them all correctly. As he leaves for school, his mom tells him that if he gets them all right today she will take him out for ice cream. So Adam takes the test, but he is a little nervous. When he gets the paper back he notices that he missed one word because he didn't put two *s's* in the word *dessert*.

Role-players: Adam, Sam, and the mother

CUE CARD 5

Allison wants to go swimming, but her stepmother says she has to clean up her room and practice the piano before she can go. Allison quickly makes her bed, picks up her dirty clothes, and dusts her dresser. She shoves a few toys under the bed and rushes downstairs to practice. She gets through the first song and starts on the second one. She is playing fast and keeps missing notes, but she doesn't stop because she is in a hurry to go. Just when she is finishing her last song, her dad walks in and tells her to play it again because he knows she is not playing the right notes. So Allison starts over and goes more slowly. She only misses a few notes this time.

Role-players: Allison, the stepmother, and the dad

All about Me

Developmental Perspective

As children become more aware of their abilities, they may become self-critical. Because they think very concretely, they tend to rate themselves as "good" or "bad" and fail to take into account that they have strengths and limitations in many areas. It is important to help children look at the total picture rather than rating themselves in just one area.

Objectives

▷ To identify strengths and weaknesses in the areas of physical, social, and intellectual development

▷ To learn not to base one's worth on a single aspect of performance

Materials

▷ Three copies of the All about Me–Diagram (Handout 2) and a pencil for each child

Procedure

1. To introduce this lesson, invite children to share about a time when they have done something physically that they have been very proud of, such as run very fast, make a good catch, or shoot a good basket. Then ask them to think about a time when they didn't do something very well. Invite them to share these experiences. Discuss the fact that everyone does some things well and other things not so well, but that doing things well does not mean you are a good person and doing things not very well does not mean you are a bad person.

2. Distribute the All about Me–Diagrams (Handout 2), three per child. Ask children to take out their pencils. On the first circle they should write the word *physical* at the top. On the second circle they should write the word *social,* and on the third circle, the word *intellectual* (for example, school performance, decision making).

3. Ask children to start with the *physical* sheet. Beside each of the plus signs, they are to write down things they do well in the physical area. Beside the minus signs, they are to write down physical things they don't do very well or could do better. Have them do the same for the *social* circle and the *intellectual* circle. For example, they may be able to run well (physical plus) but can't catch well (physical minus). In the social area, they may be able to make friends easily (social plus) but don't always cooperate (social minus). In the intellectual area, they may be a whiz in math (intellectual plus) but have a hard time with spelling (intellectual minus).

4. When children are finished, divide them into groups of three to share their responses, then discuss the Content and Personalization Questions.

Discussion

CONTENT QUESTIONS

1. Which was easier for you to think about: what you do well or what you don't do so well? How did you feel thinking about things you do well? Don't do as well?

2. Which area (physical, social, intellectual) was the most difficult for you to identify strengths and/or limitations?

3. Why do you think it is important to look at things you do well and things you don't do as well?

PERSONALIZATION QUESTIONS

1. Suppose you are not very good at anything involving physical activity. Does this mean you are not good at anything at all?

2. Suppose you are not very good at something intellectual, such as math, or something social, such as being friendly. What would this say about you? Would it mean that you aren't good at anything at all?

3. What can you tell yourself so you don't put yourself down if you are not as good in some things as you would like to be?

4. If you have limitations in some areas, are there things you can do to improve? If you never improved, would this mean you were a rotten person?

Follow-up Activity

Invite children to set a doable goal to improve something in one of these areas, but also to practice saying to themselves that they are OK even if they aren't good at it.

All about Me

DIAGRAM

Name: _____ Date: _____

_____

$-$ $+$

$+$ $+$ $-$

$-$ $-$ $+$

$+$ $+$ $-$

$-$

Stamp of Approval

Developmental Perspective

Peers become an increasingly important part of children's world at this stage of development. Peer approval, as well as approval from teachers and parents, is very important. However, it is also important to help children win their own approval without being dependent on others' approval and to help them see that others' approval does not make them more worthwhile.

Objectives

▷ To recognize ways to get approval from others and ways to approve of oneself

▷ To learn that others' approval is not required to be worthwhile

Materials

▷ A sheet of paper and a rubber stamp that spells *approved*

▷ A soda bottle

▷ A paper bag

▷ A copy of the Stamp of Approval–Categories (Handout 3)

▷ A sheet of paper and a pencil for each child

▷ Crayons and a copy of the Stamp of Approval–Certificate (Handout 4) for each child (for the Follow-up Activity)

Procedure

1. Introduce the lesson by holding up a sheet of paper with the word *approved* stamped on it. Discuss the meaning of this word: to think favorably about something, to think it is good. Explain that it is possible to get approval from a number of different sources: self, parents, teachers, and so forth.

2. Next have children sit on the floor in a circle. Show them the paper bag in which you have placed the Stamp of Approval–Categories (Handout 3).

3. Ask for two volunteers: Explain that Volunteer 1 will spin the bottle, and Volunteer 2 will reach into the bag and draw a slip of paper on which a category is written. After Volunteer 1 spins, the child to whom the bottle points responds to the category read by Volunteer 2. For example, if the category is *approval from mother,* the child will suggest something he or she might do or a way he or she might act to get approval in that category, such as offering to watch the baby while Mom runs an errand. After that child has answered, Volunteer 1 spins again, and another child responds to this same category. This procedure continues, with Volunteer 2 drawing again and two children responding to the new category, until all the slips have been drawn from the bag.

4. After the activity is finished, ask children to write a short story about someone their age who never got approval from anyone. Ask them to address these things:

   ► How would they feel if they never got anyone's approval?

   ► What would it mean about them if no one ever approved of what they did or how they acted? Would they be worthless?

   ► How could they give themselves approval if others didn't?

5. Allow time for children to share their stories in groups of four, or have them read their stories aloud to the total group.

6. Process the activity by discussing the Content and Personalization Questions.

Discussion

CONTENT QUESTIONS

1. What do you think it means if you never receive approval from anyone? Is there anything you can do to change this?

2. Suppose someone tells you that you are a rotten, no-good kid if you never get approval from others. Do you think this is true? Why or why not?

3. Do you think that someone else's approval *makes* you worthwhile? Why or why not?

4. Do you think it is important to give yourself approval?

PERSONALIZATION QUESTIONS

1. Do you receive a lot of approval from others?

2. What are some things you do to try to gain others' approval?

3. Do you ever put yourself down and think you're no good if you don't get others' approval? If so, what is something you need to remember so you don't depend on others' approval for your self-worth?

4. Do you approve of yourself? (Invite children to share examples of how they give themselves approval.)

Follow-up Activity

Use the rubber stamp and stamp the word *approved* on each child's hand. Then give each child a Stamp of Approval–Certificate (Handout 4). Have children fill in their names and two or three of their best qualities, then decorate the certificate to take home to share with family members.

Stamp of Approval

CATEGORIES

Leader note: Cut apart, then place slips in a paper bag. "Approval from yourself" intentionally appears three times.

Approval from yourself

Approval from a friend

Approval from yourself

Approval from a baby-sitter

Approval from yourself

Approval from a grandparent

Approval from your mother

Approval from an older kid

Approval from your father

Approval from a neighbor

Approval from a team member
(in a game, on a team)

Approval from a minister,
priest, or rabbi

Approval from a music teacher
(piano, other instrument)

Approval from an older
brother or sister

Approval from a leader
(Girl Scouts, Boy Scouts, 4H)

Approval from a younger
brother or sister

Approval from a stepparent

Approval from a pet

Approval from a teacher

Approval from another student

Stamp of Approval
CERTIFICATE

This Certificate of Approval recognizes

_____

as a <u>FANTASTIC</u> 4th grader who is

_____

_____

_____

I Am Someone Who...

Developmental Perspective

During this period of development, cognitive changes and an expanding social world contribute significantly to children's personality development. As they experience new things, they continually revise and extend their self-perceptions. Learning to identify personal characteristics enhances their self-development.

Objective

▷ To learn more about individual preferences, characteristics, and abilities

Materials

▷ One chair per child

▷ Paper and pencil for each child (for the Follow-up Activity)

Procedure

1. Divide the group in half and have each child take a chair. Have Group 1 members place their chairs in a straight line and Group 2 members place their chairs in a line directly across. Allow ample space in each line between chairs.

2. Ask children to sit, then pull their chairs up close enough so they are directly across from a partner. Designate one line *A* and the other line *B*. Explain that you will be giving them a discussion topic. First, all children in line *A* will talk (at the same time) to their partners about the topic for 30 seconds (you will call "time"), then it will be line *B's* turn to respond to their partners about the same topic. When the 30 seconds are up, have the children in line *A* move down one chair so everyone has a new partner. Repeat the procedure until all topics have been addressed.

DISCUSSION TOPICS

► My favorite thing to do on Saturday is ...

► One of my favorite foods is ...

► Something I worry about is ...

► Something I've never done but I'd like to do is ...

► Something I'm good at is ...

► Something I'm not good at is ...

► Something I have in common with other kids my age is ...

► A way in which I am different from other kids my age is ...

► One of my prized possessions is ...

► I like being this age because ...

- ► A mistake I've made is . . .
- ► Something I've done that I am really proud of is . . .
- ► Something that is hard for me to do is . . .
- ► Something I am good at in school is . . .
- ► Something I could improve on in school is . . .
- ► My favorite color is . . .
- ► If I could be an animal I'd be . . . because . . .
- ► I like being a (boy or girl) because . . .
- ► Something I think I'd like to be when I grow up is . . .
- ► If my house caught on fire, something I'd like to save is . . .
- ► One of my favorite ways to spend time is . . .
- ► Something I just don't think I can live without is . . .

3. Process the activity by asking the Content and Personalization Questions.

Discussion

CONTENT QUESTIONS

1. How did you feel about participating in this activity?
2. Was it hard for you to think about what to say? Were any topics more difficult for you than others?
3. Were your answers similar to your partners'? In what areas were there differences?

PERSONALIZATION QUESTIONS

1. Did you learn some new things about yourself as you thought about your responses to these topics? (Invite sharing.)
2. Based on what you shared in the activity, can you identify three words or phrases that accurately describe who you are? What are these?

Follow-up Activity

Invite students to write an "I Am Someone Who . . ." story or poem.

Tease Tolerance

Developmental Perspective

Because peers play an increasingly important role in children's lives, helping children learn to deal with the negative feelings frequently associated with peer teasing is essential. While it would be nice if children didn't tease each other, the reality is that they do. Rather than allowing children who are teased to become the victims of their hurt feelings, it is preferable to help them develop "Tease Tolerance." If their negative feelings are minimized, it will be easier for them to identify alternatives to cope with the situation.

Objective

▷ To learn effective ways to deal with feelings about being teased

Materials

▷ An ugly mask

▷ A hand mirror

▷ Paper and pencil for each child (for the Follow-up Activity)

Procedure

1. Put on the mask. Invite children to tell you how you look. Solicit words such as *ugly, dumb, terrible,* and so forth.

2. Next ask children how they might feel if someone calls them names such as ugly, dumb, and so on.

3. Tell children that you are going to help them learn that if someone calls them names or teases them, they don't have to have bad feelings. That doesn't mean that they will like being teased, just that they don't *have* to be very upset about it. The technique is called Tease Tolerance, and it goes like this:

   ▶ Someone calls you a name, like "ugly pig."

   ▶ You look in the mirror and ask yourself: "Am I ugly? Am I a pig?"

   ▶ If the answer is no, you say to yourself: "I am not ugly, and I'm not a pig because I don't have pink skin and a snout. So if I'm not what they say I am, why get upset?"

   ▶ If the answer is yes (that you are what they say you are), you still don't have to get upset about it because it may be just one or a few people who are saying these things, and it doesn't mean you are a no-good kid just because someone calls you a name.

4. Have a pair of children demonstrate the technique. In front of the group, have one child tease or call the other a name. Then help that child practice the Tease Tolerance technique just described.

5. Repeat this procedure with several volunteers, then discuss the Content and Personalization Questions.

Discussion

CONTENT QUESTIONS

1. If someone calls someone else a name, does that mean it is true?

2. What is the Tease Tolerance technique?

3. Even if what someone teases you about is true (like if they say you are stupid in math and you don't get good grades in math) what can you tell yourself so that you won't get so upset?

PERSONALIZATION QUESTIONS

1. Have you been called names before? If so, how did you feel about this?

2. Have you ever used the Tease Tolerance technique? If so, did it work for you?

3. Are there other things you have used to handle your feelings about being teased? (Invite sharing of ideas.)

Follow-up Activity

Have children write a story about when they have been teased. Have them write two endings for the story. In the first ending, have them write about what they did (or might have done) that would not be a good way to handle their feelings about teasing. In the second ending, have them write about what they did or could have done to handle their feelings about teasing in a better way. Provide opportunities for them to share the stories with others.

War on Worries

Developmental Perspective

Feeling worried is not at all uncommon for intermediate-grade children. Many of these worries relate to normal developmental experiences, while others relate to situational factors associated with moving, parental divorce or separation, money, or violence or abuse. At this age, children often do not have adequate coping mechanisms. In addition, because of their level of cognitive development, they may not see all aspects of a situation, which could help them deal more effectively with their feelings. Teaching children how to assess situations and develop ways to deal with these worries is important for their emotional growth.

Objective

▷ To learn effective strategies for dealing with worries

Materials

▷ A copy of the War on Worries–Story (Handout 5). This can be read to the children or they can each have a copy to read, depending on ability.

Procedure

1. Prior to reading the story, discuss the fact that from time to time, everyone worries. Ask children to think of a recent time they have felt worried. Invite them to share the worry with a partner or the entire group.

2. After some sharing time, invite them to read or listen to the War on Worries–Story (Handout 5) to learn new ways to deal with worries.

3. To process the activity, ask the Content and Personalization Questions.

Discussion

CONTENT QUESTIONS

1. How did the teacher help Trevor deal with his worries about his dad?
2. What did Trevor learn from the teacher?

PERSONALIZATION QUESTIONS

1. Have you ever had worries similar to Trevor's? If so, what helped you learn to worry less?
2. What advice would you give to a friend who is worried about something? How would you suggest that he or she "attack" these worries?

Follow-up Activity

Invite children to identify a worry and use the "worry line" strategy described in the story to identify ways of assessing the situation and reducing the degree of worry.

War on Worries

STORY–PAGE 1

Trevor, a fourth grader, was having trouble getting to sleep at night. Whenever he closed his eyes and tried to fall asleep, all he could think about was that something bad was going to happen to his dad. Sometimes Trevor thought his dad might get very sick and die, but most of the time he worried about his dad's getting into a serious car accident. Although he mostly thought about this at bedtime, he also worried while he was at school. If his dad didn't pick him up exactly on time, Trevor immediately thought his dad had been in an accident.

Trevor didn't want his teacher, Ms. Capella, or his friends to make fun of him because of his worries, so he tried to keep them to himself. One day, however, his dad was more than just a few minutes late, and Trevor was scared to death. He kept going back into the classroom and asking his teacher if he could use the phone to call home. Finally, his teacher said, "Trevor, you seem very worried. Are you afraid that something has happened to your dad?" Trevor burst into tears and told the teacher how worried he had been recently. Ms. Capella listened to Trevor and then told him that it is not at all uncommon to worry about these things at this age. However, Ms. Capella suggested that it might help if Trevor could talk about it and perhaps together they could find some ways to help him manage his worries.

After Trevor described what he thought might happen to his dad, Ms. Capella took out a sheet of paper and drew a line down the center of it. She asked Trevor to identify the very worst possible thing that could happen, which was that his dad would get in a terrible accident and die. Ms. Capella wrote this at one end of the line. Then she asked Trevor what the best possible thing would be, and Trevor said that his dad wouldn't be in an accident at all. Ms. Capella wrote this down on the other end of the line. Then she explained to Trevor that there are other possibilities: His dad could get in an accident but not get hurt, or he could be in an accident and get hurt but recover, for example. Ms. Capella invited Trevor to think of some other possibilities, and Trevor thought that the car could get hurt but his dad would just get a scratch. Trevor and Ms. Capella discussed where all these possibilities should be placed on the line.

War on Worries

STORY–PAGE 2

Once the line was completed, Ms. Capella helped Trevor see that one of the reasons he was worrying so much is that he saw only two possibilities: His dad would either die, or he wouldn't be in an accident at all. Ms. Capella also explained to Trevor that it was important to look into the past: Had his dad been in a serious accident before? Even if he had, he had obviously lived and was fine. Ms. Capella stressed to Trevor that it was important to look at all of this if he didn't want to be worried about everything. After Ms. Capella explained this, Trevor felt a lot better. He decided to keep the sheet of paper with him to remind him not to think only about the best or the worst.

The next day Trevor didn't worry so much about his dad, but he was worried about his schoolwork. He decided to use what Ms. Capella had taught him and see if it could work with this problem, too. He sat down and drew a line and identified the different positions. He realized that he had been thinking the worst, and that there were lots of other possibilities. After writing all the possibilities on the line, he felt a lot better. He thought he might even be able to use this idea if he had problems with his friends. Trevor was glad that he had learned a new way to attack his worries.

I Can't Do It

Developmental Perspective

Children at this age often worry about their school performance: Will they do well? Will they understand instructions? Will they get good scores on tests? Are they as smart as their classmates? It is especially important during this period of development to minimize competition and to group children as much as possible in ways that don't label some as "smarter than" others. This can help reduce some of the anxiety about school performance.

Objective

▷ To learn effective strategies to reduce negative thoughts and feelings about school performance

Materials

▷ Chalkboard

▷ A roll of masking tape

▷ A newsprint version (or an overhead transparency) of the I Can't Do It–Poster 1 (Handout 6) and the I Can't Do It–Poster 2 (Handout 7)

▷ A copy of the I Can't Do It–Game Board (Handout 8) per partnership

▷ A set of I Can't Do It–Game Cards (Handout 9), in an envelope, and two game pieces (for example, different-colored paper clips) per partnership

Procedure

1. Introduce the lesson by writing the following on the chalkboard:

   ► Missed 10 out of 12 questions on the science test.

   ► Left an important paper at home.

   ► Forgot to do the last part of the assignment.

   ► Read a paragraph aloud and didn't know how to pronounce several words.

   Ask children if they have ever experienced one or more of these events, and if so, how they felt. Next display the I Can't Do It–Poster 1 (Handout 6) and explain to children that when they feel mad, sad, stupid, or upset about situations similar to the examples given, it is because they are telling themselves something. Point to the different self-statements on the poster or transparency and ask children if they can think of other negative things they say to themselves about their school performance.

2. Next explain to children that they don't have to continue to have bad feelings about school performance or other situations because they can change the messages inside their heads. Display the I Can't Do It–Poster 2 (Handout 7) and point to the messages. Invite children to compare and contrast the messages on the two posters.

3. Ask children to find a partner, then distribute an I Can't Do It–Game Board (Handout 8), an envelope of I Can't Do It–Game Cards (Handout 9), and two game pieces to each partnership. Explain that partners are to take turns drawing a card. If the instructions on the card say to *move ahead,* they should read the situation on the card and come up with something positive they can tell themselves so they won't get down on themselves in this area of school performance. If they draw a *move back* card, they must identify an example of the negative self-talk that creates bad feelings about school performance. Refer them to the two posters and the discussion at the beginning of the lesson for examples of the two types of self-statements.

4. Allow time for children to play the game, then discuss the Content and Personalization Questions.

Discussion

CONTENT QUESTIONS

1. Think about the times you had to move back in the game. What are some examples of those negative self-statements?

2. Think about the times you were able to move ahead. What are some examples of those positive self-statements?

3. How do you think the positive self-statements could help you deal with negative feelings about school performance or other problems?

PERSONALIZATION QUESTIONS

1. Have you ever had some of the negative thoughts and feelings that were identified in the game? Do you ever think that you can't do something?

2. How do you feel when you think you can't do something or when you are learning something new and it is hard?

3. What are some examples of things you can tell yourself to keep from giving up or feeling upset about your school performance?

Follow-up Activity

Work with children to make up a song or poem to help them learn not to get upset with themselves or put themselves down about their school performance. An example follows:

> Tomorrow is my spelling test.
> I will try to do my best.
> But if I miss some
> I know I'm not dumb–
> I'll just have to try harder with the rest.

I Can't Do It

POSTER 1

I Can't Do It

POSTER 2

I Can't Do It

GAME BOARD

Instructions: As partners, take turns drawing a card from the envelope. If the card says move ahead, *give an example of positive self-talk and move your game piece the number of spaces indicated on the card. If the card says* move back, *give an example of negative self-talk and move your game piece the number of spaces indicated on the card.*

Start   **Finish**

1	**16**
2	**15**
3	**14**
4	**13**
5	**12**

6	**7**	**8**	**9**	**10**	**11**

I Can't Do It

GAME CARDS

Leader note: Cut apart cards and place in an envelope; give each partnership one set.

Yesterday you had a spelling test over all the words in the unit. The words are really hard, and you are worried.

MOVE AHEAD 2

The math worksheet you are working on looks hard.
You don't understand what to do.

MOVE BACK 2

You forgot to do some of your math problems.

MOVE BACK 1

The teacher announces that team leaders will be choosing teams for kickball. You are afraid that everyone else will get picked before you do.

MOVE AHEAD 1

You are in reading group.
The teacher asks you to read aloud, and you are afraid you won't be able to read all the words.

MOVE AHEAD 3

You have a new story to read, and there are lots of hard words.
You feel a little scared.

MOVE AHEAD 3

You don't understand the instructions for the reading worksheet, but you are afraid to ask the teacher because she might think you are dumb.

MOVE BACK 1

You miss two words on your science test.

MOVE BACK 2

Your teacher just returned an art project that you worked on last week. You got one star on yours, and the boy sitting ahead of you got two stars. You start to get down on yourself.

MOVE AHEAD 2

At recess, they are picking teams for a game. Almost everyone gets chosen before you do.

MOVE AHEAD 2

Solutions for Sad Feelings

Developmental Perspective

Depending on their circumstances, children this age may frequently experience sad feelings. Because they are still in the process of developing a feelings vocabulary and learning ways to express feelings, they may not be able to identify effective ways to deal with their sadness. The lessons learned in this activity will help children identify specific things they can do to help themselves feel less sad.

Objectives

▷ To identify specific ways to deal with sad feelings

Materials

▷ A Solutions for Sad Feelings–Worksheet (Handout 10) and a pencil for every two children

▷ Poster paper and a marker

Procedure

1. Divide children into pairs.

2. Distribute the Solutions for Sad Feelings–Worksheet (Handout 10) to each pair of children. Explain that you will be reading some sad situations, and their job is to think of ways to help the child in the situation feel less sad. After reading the first situation, allow partners a short amount of time to discuss what they could do to deal with the sad feelings (they can write this on the worksheet or just talk about ideas). Then ask them to share these ideas with the total group. As they share, write their suggestions on the poster paper.

3. Read the next situation and follow the same procedure until all have been addressed, then discuss the Content and Personalization Questions.

Discussion

CONTENT QUESTIONS

1. Do you think everyone feels sad about the same things? If not, why do you think they don't?

2. Were you surprised at the number of different ideas you came up with to deal with sad feelings?

3. Do you think it is possible to feel less sad about sad situations if you find some good ways to help you deal with them?

PERSONALIZATION QUESTIONS

1. Have you tried any of the ideas that were suggested today? If so, which ones have worked best for you?

2. Of the ideas presented today, which ones would you like to try the next time you feel sad?

Follow-up Activity

Keep the composite list posted where children can see it. At the end of the day, ask children if they felt sad and, if so, which suggestions they tried.

Solutions for Sad Feelings

WORKSHEET

SITUATION 1

Carlos's dog, who was 8 years old, just got run over by a car. What could you suggest that might help Carlos feel less sad?

_____

_____

_____

_____

SITUATION 2

Annie's grandmother fell and broke her leg. She is in the hospital. What could you suggest that might help Annie feel less sad?

_____

_____

_____

_____

SITUATION 3

Miguel's sister ran away from home. She called her parents and told them she got a job in another city and wasn't ever coming back. What could you suggest that might help Miguel feel less sad?

_____

_____

_____

_____

SITUATION 4

Theresa's best friend is moving to another town. What could you suggest that might help Theresa feel less sad?

_____

_____

_____

_____

SITUATION 5

Demi's dad is in prison. She hasn't seen him for a long time. What could you suggest to help Demi feel less sad?

_____

_____

_____

_____

SITUATION 6

Daryl's family has to move because they can't afford to live in the house they are living in now. Daryl doesn't want to move out of his neighborhood. What could you suggest that might help Daryl feel less sad?

_____

_____

_____

_____

Together We Can

Developmental Perspective

As children enter the latter part of middle childhood and become more active in team sports and group activities, it is not unusual for competition to increase. Competition can have negative aspects in that some children will do whatever they can to be "the best." Relationships can become strained if children resort to put-downs and other negative behaviors to maintain their status. Because they will need to work with others throughout life, children must develop skills to work cooperatively.

Objective

▷ To enhance skills in working cooperatively with others

Materials

▷ A paper bag for each group of five children. Each bag should contain 6–8 objects for children to incorporate into a skit about friendship–for example, a ball, a glove, age-appropriate toys, books, tapes or CD's, stuffed animals, an item of clothing, school supplies, and videos. (Objects do not have to be the same for each bag.)

▷ A copy of the Together We Can–Observer Checklist (Handout 11) and a pencil for each group observer

▷ Blocks (or newspapers and a roll of masking tape; for the Follow-up Activity)

Procedure

1. Introduce the lesson by asking children to suggest something they think they could do better if they worked in a group as opposed to working alone.

2. After several examples have been shared, divide children into groups of five (four participants and one observer) and distribute a paper bag of objects to each group. Explain that each group's task is to use all of the objects in the bag to create a short skit to demonstrate some aspect of friendship.

3. Ask each group to select an observer. Give each observer a Together We Can–Observer Checklist (Handout 11). Explain that the observers will look for examples of the types of behaviors indicated on the sheet and check them off as they occur. These sheets should *not* be shown to other group members.

4. Give children planning and practice time, then have them present their skits to the total group. After the skits, discuss the Content and Personalization Questions.

Discussion

CONTENT QUESTIONS

1. How did your group decide what to do?

2. Did you or anyone else in your group have to compromise in order to cooperate? If so, was this easy or difficult?

3. Do you think members of your group cooperated with each other? If so, what were some examples of these cooperative behaviors?

4. Do you think you could have come up with ideas for this skit by yourself, or was it better to work together?

PERSONALIZATION QUESTIONS

1. When you work in a group, do you cooperate with others? If not, what is difficult for you about cooperation?

2. Did you learn anything today about cooperating that will help you at school, at home, or when you are with friends? If so, what did you learn and how will you apply it?

Follow-up Activity

Give small groups another cooperative task, such as building a tower out of blocks or making a bridge out of newspapers and masking tape. Assign an observer to each group to record examples of cooperative behavior.

Together We Can

OBSERVER CHECKLIST

	Observed	Not observed
Group members shared ideas.	☐	☐
Group members cooperated.	☐	☐
Group members said good things about other members' ideas.	☐	☐
Group members all took part in the project. No one was left out.	☐	☐
Group members listened to one another.	☐	☐
Group members compromised.	☐	☐
Group members argued or fought.	☐	☐
Group members couldn't agree on ideas.	☐	☐

Don't Bully Me

Developmental Perspective

During middle childhood it is not uncommon for children to feel intimidated by bullying behavior. Skill development and emotional self-management need to be introduced and practiced so children can more effectively deal with this kind of behavior.

Objectives

▷ To define bullying

▷ To learn effective ways to deal with bullying behavior

Materials

▷ A copy of the Don't Bully Me–Scenarios (Handout 12) for each child

▷ Several sheets of newsprint, a marker, and a roll of masking tape

▷ A small paper plate, crayons or markers, and a safety pin for each child

Procedure

1. Ask children to define what they think a *bully* is (someone who pushes others around, who intimidates or picks on others who might be weaker). Emphasize that bullying is something anyone is capable of doing and that bullying can occur in varying degrees; some kids may occasionally bully others, and others may act like bullies almost all the time. Indicate that the purpose of this lesson is to identify ways to help children avoid being affected by bullying behavior or becoming a bully.

2. Distribute the Don't Bully Me–Scenarios (Handout 12) to each child. Ask children to read each scenario and complete the first two questions. Then assign children to groups of three and have them brainstorm what the children in these scenarios could have done to defend themselves against the bullying and list these responses under the third question on each worksheet.

3. After groups have completed their brainstorming, discuss the bullying behaviors and the group's ideas about what can be done to defend against bullying. List these ideas on a sheet of newsprint so they can be posted and referred to as needed.

4. Distribute a small paper plate, crayons or markers, and a safety pin to each child. Invite children to make an "I'm Not a Bully" badge or a "Don't Bully Me" badge incorporating the ideas discussed in their groups. If they choose to wear the badge, it is their "contract" not to bully others or their reminder of what they can do to defend themselves against bullying.

5. To process the activity, discuss the Content and Personalization Questions.

Discussion

CONTENT QUESTIONS

1. What is bullying?
2. Why do you think some children bully others?
3. What can you do to defend yourself against bullies?

PERSONALIZATION QUESTIONS

1. Has anyone ever bullied you? If so, how did you feel about it?
2. What can you do to try and prevent others from bullying you?
3. If you can't prevent others from bullying you, what can you do once it has happened? Whom can you go to for help?
4. Did you learn anything from this lesson that you can use if you have a problem with being a bully or being bullied? (Invite sharing.)

Follow-up Activity

Have children work in small groups and prepare a short presentation to give to younger students about bullying and how to defend against it.

Don't Bully Me

SCENARIOS–PAGE 1

Name: _____ Date: _____

SCENARIO 1

Allison and Amy were walking home from the library. As they turned the corner, Allison noticed two older girls coming up close behind them. She recognized one of them as being in her sister's class. Pretty soon one of the older girls started walking faster and kept stepping on Amy's heels. Amy turned around and asked her to please stop. The older girl laughed and kept doing it. Allison and Amy were afraid . . . they didn't know why these girls were doing this, but it was getting worse. Then all of a sudden the older girl gave Allison and Amy a hard shove and ran off laughing and yelling, "So long, little wimps."

1. Bullying behaviors: _____

_____

_____

2. What did Allison and Amy do to defend themselves against these girls? _____

_____

_____

3. What else do you think they could have done? _____

_____

_____

Don't Bully Me

SCENARIOS–PAGE 2

SCENARIO 2

Corey was riding his bike in the neighborhood and thought he would stop and see his friend Adam. As he rode up to Adam's house, Adam's older brother walked out of the garage and blocked Corey's path. "What do you think you are doing on my property, kid?" bellowed Adam's brother. "I just wanted to see if Adam was home," said Corey. "Well, he's not, and I'm not about to let him play with you. Get out of here. If I see you near here again, you'll be sorry."

1. Bullying behaviors: _____

_____

_____

2. What did Corey do to defend himself against Adam's brother?_____

_____

_____

3. What else do you think he could have done? _____

_____

_____

Don't Bully Me

SCENARIOS–PAGE 3

SCENARIO 3

Charlie sat behind Ann at school. Every day he would stare at her, say mean things to her, and threaten to beat her up after school. Ann was scared, so she always made sure she had a friend to walk home with. One day she had to stay after school, so there was no one to walk home with. She left the classroom and walked to the front door of the school. As she opened it, she saw Charlie and his friend waiting for her. She quickly stepped back inside and ran down the hall to another door. She opened it and peeked outside. She didn't see the two boys, so she ran as fast as she could to the end of the block. All of a sudden she heard them yell and knew they were behind her. She ran faster and faster, and just managed to make it to her yard before they caught up with her. Her mother was standing by the window, so the boys left, but they told her they'd "get her" later.

1. Bullying behaviors: _____

_____

_____

2. What did Ann do to defend herself against the boys? _____

_____

_____

3. What else do you think she could have done?_____

_____

_____

Don't Bully Me

SCENARIOS–PAGE 4

SCENARIO 4

Phillip and Pam were riding their bikes home from school. Suddenly, Phillip felt someone crash into the back of his bike. He turned around and recognized a fifth grader. At first Phillip thought the boy had accidentally run into him, but the fifth grader said, "Get out of my way. We don't want you on this street." Pam said, "We have a right to be here, too. We're not doing anything wrong." The kid just glared at her and told her to shut up. "This is my neighborhood, and if you don't get out of here, I'll make it worse for you."

1. Bullying behaviors: _____

_____

_____

2. What did Phillip and Pam do to defend themselves? _____

_____

_____

3. What else do you think they could have done? _____

_____

_____

Pointers for Put-Downs

Developmental Perspective

Because social interaction increases during middle childhood, so do interpersonal conflicts. At this age, children are becoming more competitive and are more concerned about how they measure up to others. Some have not mastered perspective taking. These factors all contribute to put-down behaviors, which can have a negative impact on self-acceptance.

Objectives

▷ To develop skills in dealing with put-downs from others

▷ To learn that one's worth as a person is not contingent on what others say about one

Materials

▷ Chalkboard

▷ Tagboard labels of the following words: *stupid, ugly, wimp, loser, fatso*

▷ A roll of masking tape

▷ A 3 × 5–inch index card and a pencil for each child

Procedure

1. Introduce the lesson by selecting five volunteers. Ask them to stand and face the rest of the group. Tape one of the tagboard labels on each of their backs. Volunteers should not see their labels, nor should other children at this point.

2. Ask children in the group to tell you three things about each volunteer. List these characteristics on the chalkboard under each child's name. After all adjectives have been listed, ask volunteers to turn around to display their labels. Ask children if the words on the board correspond to the labels. Emphasize the fact that some children use these labels to put others down, but that the labels are seldom true, as this activity has just demonstrated.

3. Next divide children into groups of five and have them make up a skit to illustrate the concept of put-downs, what children think and feel when others put them down, and how to deal with put-downs. Allow time for planning, then have children present their skits.

4. Introduce the concept of *self-talk* as a way to deal with put-downs. Explain that self-talk is what you can say to yourself so you won't be as upset by the put-downs. Examples:

    ▶ Sticks and stones can break my bones but words can't hurt me unless I let them.

> ▶ Am I what they say I am?
>
> ▶ I don't like what they are saying, but I can handle this without getting upset because I know that what they are saying isn't true.
>
> ▶ Getting mad will just show them they are getting to me.

5. Distribute the index cards and pencils, one per child. Ask children to think of other examples of self-talk and create catchy "slogans" to help them remember these messages. Have children write these slogans on the index cards to help remind them of what they can say the next time they feel put down by others.

6. Provide time for children to share their slogans, then discuss the Content and Personalization Questions.

Discussion

CONTENT QUESTIONS

1. Do you think put-downs are common?
2. Why do you think children put others down?
3. Just because someone puts you down, are you what that person says you are?

PERSONALIZATION QUESTIONS

1. The next time someone puts you down, how can you handle it so you don't get very upset?
2. Have you ever used self-talk as a way to deal with put-downs? If so, how did it work for you?
3. Did you learn anything from this lesson that you can apply to your relationships with others?

Follow-up Activity

Ask children to continue to create self-talk slogans and to practice self-talk if they experience a put-down.

Rules for Relationships

Developmental Perspective

As children mature and expand their social networks, they will inevitably encounter people who will mistreat them in some way. While it would be preferable if everyone treated others in a positive manner, it is usually not possible to control others. Therefore, helping children identify effective skills to deal with negative relationship issues is a way to empower them.

Objectives

▷ To identify effective coping skills to deal with others' mistreatment

▷ To learn what one can and cannot control in interpersonal situations

Materials

▷ A Rules for Relationships–Game Board (Handout 13) for each group of four children

▷ A different-colored paper clip or another type of game piece for each child within a group

▷ An envelope containing four small slips of paper, numbered 1–4, for each group

▷ Six sheets of newsprint, labeled as follows:

Effective ways to handle it if someone *teases* you

Effective ways to handle it if someone *rejects* you

Effective ways to handle it if someone *pushes* you or *hurts* you

Effective ways to handle it if someone *laughs* at you

Effective ways to handle it if someone *calls you a name*

Effective ways to handle it if someone *starts a fight* with you

▷ A roll of masking tape and a marker

Procedure

1. Engage children in a general discussion about things others do that they don't like. (Stress that no names should be used.) Talk with children about the fact that although the world would undoubtedly be a better place if everyone treated them the way they would like to be treated, this is often not the way it is in reality. Ask children to raise a hand if they think they are usually successful in preventing other children from calling them names, teasing them, laughing at them, and so forth. Ask them who they *can* control if they can't stop others from doing these kinds of things. Indicate that the purpose of this lesson is to help them identify things they can think, feel, or do to help them cope more effectively with negative relationships.

2. Divide children into groups of four. Distribute one Rules for Relationships–Game Board (Handout 13), four different-colored paper clips (or other game pieces), and an envelope of slips numbered 1–4 to each group. Review the instructions on the game board.

3. Allow sufficient time for children to play the game, then discuss the Content Questions. As children give suggestions for each question, list these on the separate sheets of newsprint.

4. Review the information from Activity 3, "Pointers for Put-Downs," emphasizing the use of self-talk and the importance of not assuming that what others say is true as effective ways of reducing emotional upset and dealing with negative relationship issues.

5. Discuss the Personalization Questions.

Discussion

CONTENT QUESTIONS

1. What were some of the suggestions your group had for dealing effectively with *teasing?*

2. What were some of the suggestions your group had for dealing effectively with *being rejected* by a friend?

3. What were some of the suggestions your group had for dealing effectively with someone *pushing* you or *hurting* you?

4. What were some of the suggestions your group had for dealing effectively with someone *laughing* at you?

5. What were some of the suggestions your group had for dealing effectively with someone *calling you a name?*

6. What were some of the suggestions your group had for dealing effectively with someone who *starts a fight* with you?

PERSONALIZATION QUESTIONS

1. Have you experienced any of these situations in your relationships with friends? If so, what has worked best for you?

2. Have you ever been able to stop others from teasing you or rejecting you? If so, what did you do? If not, how did you handle it?

3. Do you usually get upset or angry when someone teases you, laughs at you, or calls you a name? Do you think it helps to get upset? Are you what other people say you are? Do you have to believe that what they are saying is true?

4. Did you learn anything from this lesson that you can use the next time someone treats you in ways you don't like to be treated? (Invite sharing.)

Follow-up Activity

Keep the newsprint sheets of suggestions posted. Invite children to try out these suggestions and at the end of the week to write a short report about how they did or did not work.

Rules for Relationships

GAME BOARD–PAGE 1

Instructions: Take turns drawing a number from the envelope and moving your game piece the number of spaces indicated. When you land, match the letter on the space with the letter on the following list. Think of a positive way you could deal with the situation.

T   Something you could do to handle *teasing*.

R   Something you could do if a friend *rejects* you.

P   Something you could do if someone *pushes* you or *hurts* you.

L   Something you could do if someone *laughs* at you.

C   Something you could do if someone *calls you a name*.

S   Something you could do if someone *starts a fight* with you.

Rules for Relationships

GAME BOARD–PAGE 2

Start **Finish**

Tunnel Vision

Developmental Perspective

Because they are concrete thinkers, children this age still take things quite literally and fail to look at a variety of perspectives. As a result, they frequently have misunderstandings with others or upset themselves because they do not see all aspects of an issue. Learning this skill is an important part of their cognitive development.

Objectives

▷ To differentiate between making an assumption and considering multiple perspectives

▷ To recognize the negative effects of making assumptions

▷ To learn how to check out assumptions

Materials

▷ One or more toy kaleidoscopes

Procedure

1. Introduce the lesson by circulating the kaleidoscopes, allowing time for exploration. Ask children if they just see one thing when they look through the kaleidoscope, or if they see lots of variety and changing patterns. Then ask children if they know what it means to put blinders on an animal: What happens to the animal's vision? Discuss the contrast between having blinders on and looking through a kaleidoscope, emphasizing that sometimes people act as if they have blinders on and see only one aspect of a situation. They usually assume that something is true and they don't bother to check it out or consider other possibilities. Introduce the term *tunnel vision,* explaining that we use this term when people act as though they have blinders on, make assumptions, and limit their thinking to one possibility. Discuss how having tunnel vision could possibly create problems at home, at school, or with friends. Stress the difference between having tunnel vision and considering a variety of perspectives, as would be the case with *kaleidoscope vision.*

2. Read the following situation aloud:

   You are at school and it is time for lunch recess. It is your turn to take the ball outside, so you go to the closet to get it. Just as you turn the corner to get to the closet, you see Kelly running out the other side of the room. It looks as though she is carrying something.

Ask students to pretend that they have tunnel vision (thinking about only one aspect of the situation and making assumptions). How would they interpret this situation if they were thinking this way? (Most will say Kelly took the ball.) Then ask them to imagine that they are looking through a kaleidoscope and seeing many different perspectives or possibilities. Ask children to share what some of these might be: that Kelly just happened to be in the room and didn't take the ball, that Kelly thought it was her day to get the ball and didn't realize she was doing something wrong, and so on. Emphasize the difference between the two ways of thinking; ask children to identify the negative consequences that could result from having tunnel vision.

3. Next divide children into two groups and have the groups stand and form two lines. Designate one group as the Tunnel Vision Group and the other as the Kaleidoscope Vision Group. Explain that you will be reading some situations. As you read each one, the first child in the Tunnel Vision Group will make an *assumption* about the situation and state it aloud. The first child in the Kaleidoscope Vision Group will state at least two different possible points of view. The child in the Tunnel Vision Group who made the assumption next checks it out by asking you to read the *fact*. If the assumption is correct, the child may remain standing but moves to the back of the line. If not, he or she sits down. The first child in the Kaleidoscope Vision Group also moves to the back of the line, and the next two players proceed in the same manner. The game continues until all situations have been read and all assumptions checked out.

TUNNEL VISION SITUATIONS

► Situation 1: Tom was supposed to be home at 5:00, but he didn't get home until 6:00. His mother assumed . . . (*Fact:* He lost his watch and didn't know what time it was.)

► Situation 2: Shiron got a bad grade on his science test. His teacher assumed . . . (*Fact:* Shiron's pet rabbit died the night before, and he was thinking about that and couldn't concentrate.)

► Situation 3: Daphne had 5 dollars on her dresser. When she got ready for bed she noticed that the money wasn't there. Daphne assumed . . . (*Fact:* The window was open and the wind had blown the money onto the floor, where she couldn't see it.)

► Situation 4: Donita didn't sit by her friend Betsy on the bus. Betsy assumed . . . (*Fact:* Donita hadn't seen the empty seat beside Betsy.)

► Situation 5: Terrance didn't go to Josh's birthday party. Josh assumed . . . (*Fact:* Terrance was grounded for lying to his mother.)

► Situation 6: Aaron didn't go to ball practice last night. The coach assumed . . . (*Fact:* Aaron decided not to play ball.)

► Situation 7: Darcy didn't call her friend Megan back after Megan had left a message with Darcy's mother asking Darcy to call her. Megan assumed . . . (*Fact:* Megan's mother didn't give her the message.)

► Situation 8: Molly ignored Serita on the playground. Serita assumed . . . (*Fact:* Molly didn't see her.)

► Situation 9: Jonathan told Ben that he would play with him after school, but when Ben called him, Jonathan was gone. Ben assumed . . . (*Fact:* Jonathan had to go somewhere with his mom and forgot to call Ben.)

► Situation 10: Javier told Gabriel that he was going out of town for the weekend. On Saturday Gabriel saw Javier on the city bus. Gabriel assumed . . . (*Fact:* Javier's mother changed her mind.)

► Situation 11: Terri never invited any of the girls over to play or stay overnight at her house. The girls assumed . . . (*Fact:* Terri's mother drinks too much, and Terri is embarrassed to have anyone over.)

► Situation 12: Jessica got a terrible grade on her science test. The teacher assumed . . . (*Fact:* Jessica hadn't studied at all.)

4. To process the activity, ask the Content and Personalization Questions.

Discussion

CONTENT QUESTIONS

1. What is the difference between a tunnel vision thinker and a kaleidoscope thinker?

2. Which type of thinking do you believe is best?

3. In this activity, was it difficult to think of multiple perspectives?

4. In this activity, did many of the assumptions turn out to be correct? If not, what does this tell you about making assumptions?

PERSONALIZATION QUESTIONS

1. Are you more of a tunnel vision thinker or more of a kaleidoscope thinker?

2. When you make assumptions, are there ever any negative consequences? Positive consequences? (Invite sharing of examples.)

3. If you are a tunnel vision thinker, are you happy about this? If not, what can you do to change?

Follow-up Activity

Have children write a story about making assumptions and the negative things that can happen as a result. An optional activity would be to read *The True Story of the Three Little Pigs,* by John Scieszka (New York: First Scholastic Printing, 1989) and to discuss the different viewpoints.

Long & Short of It

Developmental Perspective

One of the most challenging developmental tasks is learning to consider consequences. As concrete thinkers, children at this age often have difficulty projecting beyond the present. However, they need to develop this skill in order to make good decisions.

Objectives

▷ To identify consequences

▷ To differentiate between short- and long-term consequences

Materials

▷ A Long and Short of It–Game Board (Handout 14) for each group of three children

▷ For each group, a set of answers from the Long and Short of It–Answer Sheets (Handout 15)

Procedure

1. To begin the lesson, ask for three volunteers to act out two very short role-plays. Instruct the first volunteer to pretend to be a student who comes into the classroom and announces to the teacher (a volunteer) that he or she has left the homework assignment at home. Instruct the third volunteer to pretend to be a student who sneaks into the classroom and takes a large sum of money out of the teacher's purse (or wallet) when the teacher isn't looking.

2. Ask volunteers to do the role-plays. Then engage children in a discussion about the possible consequences of each of these actions. Distinguish between short- and long-term consequences, stressing the fact that in the second role-play, the consequences could have a long-term effect if this theft went on a child's school record, he or she had to be on probation, and so on.

3. Ask children to give other examples of short- and long-term consequences to demonstrate that they understand the distinction. Then divide children into groups of three. Distribute a Long and Short of It–Game Board (Handout 14) to each group. Explain that one child is the judge, who will determine whether the response is correct. Give each judge the corresponding Long and Short of It–Answer Sheet (Handout 15). The other two players take turns selecting a square, stating whether it is a short or long-term consequence, checking it out with the judge, and marking either an *S* (for short term) or an *L* (for long term) in that square if the response was correct. The game ends when one player has three *L's* or three *S's* in a row on the board (as in tic-tac-toe). Play a total of three games so everyone has a chance to play and be the judge.

4. To process the activity, ask the Content and Personalization Questions.

Discussion

CONTENT QUESTIONS

1. What are consequences?
2. What is the difference between short- and long-term consequences?
3. Do you think it is important to consider consequences when you decide to do something?
4. Can you do anything to change consequences?
5. Which might be more difficult to change, short- or long-term consequences? Why?

PERSONALIZATION QUESTIONS

1. Which is easier for you to identify: short- or long-term consequences?
2. Are you usually good at predicting consequences? If so, do you think that makes a difference in your behavior?
3. Have you ever known anyone who wasn't good at predicting consequences? If so, what effect did that have on this person?

Follow-up Activity

Students can create their own tic-tac-toe game using short- and long-term consequences similar to those used in this lesson. Have children trade games and play, with the creator of the game acting as the judge for his or her own game.

Long & Short of It

GAME BOARDS—PAGE 1

GAME 1

Take turns choosing a square, reading what is written there, and identifying the consequences as either short term *(S)* or long term *(L)*. After each turn, the judge will let you know whether your answer is correct. If it is, mark the square *S* or *L*. The game is over when one player gets three *S*'s or three *L*'s in a row.

1. You are grounded for one day for being late for dinner.	2. You have to sit in an assigned seat on the bus for three months because you got into too many fights.	3. You have been reading without good light, and now you have to wear glasses.
4. You made cookies for your grandma, and she gave you a dollar.	5. You haven't been feeding your dog without being reminded, and yesterday you didn't feed her at all. Your dad is giving the dog away.	6. You watched TV and didn't do your homework. You had to stay in for recess to finish it.
7. You played outside without your jacket, and now you have a cold.	8. You stole some candy from the swimming pool concession stand the first day the pool opened. You can't go to the pool the rest of the summer.	9. Your brother hit you in the stomach and has to spend the rest of the evening in his room.

Long & Short of It

GAME BOARDS—PAGE 2

GAME 2

Take turns choosing a square, reading what is written there, and identifying the consequences as either short term *(S)* or long term *(L)*. After each turn, the judge will let you know whether your answer is correct. If it is, mark the square *S* or *L*. The game is over when one player gets three *S's* or three *L's* in a row.

1. Your teacher asked you to be the hall monitor for the rest of the year because you did such a good job the first two months of school.	2. Your friend shared her dessert with you today because you gave her a cookie yesterday.	3. You got a good grade on your test because you studied hard.
4. You didn't get to go out and play because you didn't study.	5. Your mom makes you go to bed early for a week for fighting about what to watch on TV.	6. You get teased by bullies because you don't go join in their mean pranks.
7. You win a prize for finding the answer to a hard question on the social studies quiz.	8. You get mad and put your fist through a glass door. Your hand is broken.	9. You are elected class president for next year because you gave a good speech.

Long & Short of It

GAME BOARDS—PAGE 3

GAME 3

Take turns choosing a square, reading what is written there, and identifying the consequences as either short term *(S)* or long term *(L)*. After each turn, the judge will let you know whether your answer is correct. If it is, mark the square *S* or *L*. The game is over when one player gets three *S's* or three *L's* in a row.

1. Other kids laughed at you because they thought you gave a stupid answer.	2. People were friendly to you because you smiled at them.	3. Your friends helped with your work because you helped them last week.
4. You got grounded for disobeying your mom.	5. You got extra dessert because you ate a good dinner.	6. Your brother did your chores for you because you helped him.
7. You can't play ball this summer because you got bad grades in science and math last year and must go to summer school.	8. You stole a kid's bike and have to work every Saturday all year to buy him a new bike.	9. You won an award for being nice to older people in the nursing home. Your award will be displayed permanently at school.

Long & Short of It

ANSWER SHEETS

Leader note: Cut each set of answers apart so judges see only the answers for the game they are judging.

GAME 1: ANSWERS	GAME 2: ANSWERS	GAME 3: ANSWERS
Players will take turns choosing a square, reading what is written there, and identifying the consequences as either short term *(S)* or long term *(L)*. After each turn, you will judge each player's answer as correct or incorrect.	Players will take turns choosing a square, reading what is written there, and identifying the consequences as either short term *(S)* or long term *(L)*. After each turn, you will judge each player's answer as correct or incorrect.	Players will take turns choosing a square, reading what is written there, and identifying the consequences as either short term *(S)* or long term *(L)*. After each turn, you will judge each player's answer as correct or incorrect.
1. Short-term	1. Long-term	1. Short-term
2. Long-term	2. Short-term	2. Short-term
3. Long-term	3. Short-term	3. Short-term
4. Short-term	4. Short-term	4. Short-term
5. Long-term	5. Short-term	5. Short-term
6. Short-term	6. Short-term	6. Short-term
7. Short-term	7. Short-term	7. Long-term
8. Long-term	8. Long-term	8. Long-term
9. Short-term	9. Long-term	9. Long-term

Really Rational

Developmental Perspective

Although at this age children are able to think more logically and reason more realistically, it is still very common for them to make assumptions, overgeneralize, and misconstrue information. Learning rational thinking skills is an important part of their cognitive development.

Objectives

▷ To understand the concept of irrational beliefs

▷ To learn to identify irrational beliefs

Materials

▷ A Really Rational–Role-Play Situation (Handout 16) for each group of four children

Procedure

1. Begin the lesson by asking for three volunteers: one to play a principal and two to play students. In private, explain to the volunteers that the principal is going to walk into the classroom dragging two students who have been in a fight on the playground. You will play the role of the teacher. When the principal brings in the students, he or she should say something like: "Can't you control these students? They were in a fight on the playground. Students shouldn't do things like this."

2. Enact the role-play. After the principal speaks to you, you say to the students:

   Oh, I am such a *horrible* teacher, and you are *horrible* students for behaving like this. Why do you *always* have to misbehave? Now the principal will *never* let my class go out on the playground, and the principal will *always* think I am a terrible teacher because I can't control my students. I should *never* have become a teacher to begin with. I know *all* the other teachers will be talking about me and *all* the students on the playground will be talking about how terrible you two are. You two *should* know how to behave by now; after all, you are in fourth grade. This is such a *bad* situation; I can't imagine anything worse.

3. Ask the children to analyze your reaction: Do they think you overreacted? If so, how? What did you say that might have been an exaggeration (blowing something out of proportion)? What did you say that was probably unrealistic? Encourage them to be specific. As a result of the discussion, identify the following irrational beliefs, illustrating with examples:

   ▶ Overgeneralizations: making it sound as though the situation is *always* this way. Examples: The principal will *never* let us go on the playground again; the principal will *always* think I am a terrible teacher.

   ▶ Exaggerations: blowing things out of proportion. Examples: *All* the teachers will talk about me and *all* the students will talk about how terrible you two are; I can't imagine a worse situation.

   ▶ Self put-downs: thinking you are terrible because of what happened. Examples: I am such a *horrible* teacher; I should *never* have become a teacher to begin with.

   ▶ "Shoulds": rigid standards for how you or others must be. Examples: You two *should* know how to behave by now.

   Emphasize that a lot of irrational beliefs contain words such as *always* or *never*. They don't reflect reality. For example, are students absolutely horrible if they get in a fight once? Is the teacher terrible because her students misbehave?

4. Ask children whether they think this kind of irrational thinking is helpful. Then demonstrate how to challenge thoughts like this through a process known as *disputing*. When you dispute, you ask yourself questions such as: "Where's the proof that I'm a terrible teacher just because two of my students got into a fight? And just because they had this trouble, does that mean *everybody* will talk about me or think I am terrible? Don't I usually do a good job as a teacher? Is this really the worst thing that could happen?

5. Divide children into groups of four. Give each group one of the Really Rational–Role-Play Situations (Handout 16). Ask groups to act out the situation by being very unrealistic and irrational. After some practice time, have children present their skits. After each one, involve the rest of the group in identifying the irrational beliefs. After all groups have presented and discussed, have each group present the skit again, this time demonstrating rational beliefs and/or disputes.

6. Process the activity by discussing the Content and Personalization Questions.

Discussion

Content Questions

1. What are some examples of irrational beliefs?
2. Do you think it is good or bad to have irrational beliefs?
3. How do you get rid of irrational beliefs?

PERSONALIZATION QUESTIONS

1. Do you or does anyone you know think these irrational thoughts?

2. When you have had irrational thoughts, did the situation turn out to be as terrible or horrible as you first thought it would be?

3. Are you successful in disputing your irrational beliefs?

Follow-up Activity

Develop a list of irrational beliefs. Have children form two lines. Read an irrational belief to the first child in Line 1 and ask him or her to give you an example of a dispute to that belief. Then ask the first child in Line 2 to give another example of a dispute for the same belief. These children then rotate to the end of the line, and the procedure continues with a different irrational belief for the next two children, and so on until all beliefs have been read and disputed.

Really Rational

ROLE-PLAY SITUATIONS

Leader note: Cut apart so each group of four receives one role-play situation.

SITUATION 1
You and your brother didn't make your beds and your dad and mom are very upset about this.
(Example: Can't you two ever do anything right?)

SITUATION 2
You and your two friends get a *C* on a science project you worked hard on. The teacher can't believe you got this grade.
(Example: We are so dumb; we'll probably flunk science.)

SITUATION 3
Your best friend sits by someone else at lunch and keeps looking over at you and the person you are sitting beside.
(Example: The person is saying awful things about me.)

SITUATION 4
Your little sister went into your room and took one of your books. You find out and are furious. You run to your parents to tell them.
(Example: She is the worst sister in the world.)

SITUATION 5
You were supposed to feed your dog, but you forgot. Your brother was supposed to change the cat litter, and he didn't do it. Your dad and your stepmom are very upset about how irresponsible the two of you are.
(Example: You are always irresponsible.)

SITUATION 6
You are in a skating club, and the trainer just taught you how to do a jump. She tells you and two other kids to try it. They get it right, and you don't.
(Example: I'll never learn this.)

Problems & Solutions

Developmental Perspective

At this stage of development, children are able to make inferences and take into account several perspectives in solving a problem. Their thinking is generally more logical, and they have a more realistic outlook. However, as they mature and are faced with more challenging problems, they need to be able to implement a problem-solving process.

Objectives

▷ To learn a problem-solving process

▷ To practice using problem-solving skills

Materials

▷ Chalkboard

▷ A box of toothpicks, a sheet of paper, and a bottle of glue for every four children

▷ A roll of masking tape

▷ A newsprint version of the Problems and Solutions–Problem-Solving Steps (Handout 17)

Procedure

1. Ask children to think of a recent problem they have had and what steps they went through to solve the problem. Elicit ideas and write the problem-solving steps on the chalkboard.

2. Indicate that the purpose of this lesson is to give children experience in practicing problem solving. Divide children into groups of four and distribute a box of toothpicks, a sheet of paper, and a bottle of glue to each group. Explain that their task as a group is to build a tower out of the toothpicks, using the paper as the base of the tower but gluing only the toothpicks at the bottom to the paper (in other words, leaving the other toothpicks in the tower unglued). Allow about 15 minutes for groups to work. Provide time for them to share their towers with the total group.

3. Next post the newsprint version of the Problems and Solutions–Problem-Solving Steps (Handout 17). Read and carefully describe each step of the process. As you do this, ask children to share specific examples of how they did or did not follow this process as they built their towers.

4. Next read aloud the following dilemma. Ask children to listen carefully. Then as a large group, work through each step of the problem-solving process as it would apply to this dilemma.

> Brad was in the store looking for a video to rent. His stepmother was in another aisle. There was a man not far from Brad who was also looking at videos. A young girl came up and asked the man (who was apparently her dad) for money to buy some candy. The man pulled out a dollar bill and gave it to her. As he did, a 5-dollar bill fell out on the floor. Brad didn't notice it right away, and just as he glanced down, he saw the man walking out of the store. Brad picked up the 5 dollars. What should he do? He had been wanting a model car . . . and the 5 dollars would pay for it. How would you solve this problem?

5. Process the activity by discussing the Content and Personalization Questions.

Discussion

CONTENT QUESTIONS

1. When you were building the tower, did you follow the steps of the problem-solving process? Which steps did your group do well? Which steps did your group not do as well?

2. Did you think it was easier or harder to apply this process to the dilemma with Brad?

3. Do you think a process like this is helpful in solving problems? Why or why not?

PERSONALIZATION QUESTIONS

1. When you have a problem to solve, do you use steps similar to the ones presented in this lesson? If so, how do they work for you in solving your "real-life" problems? How do you think using a process like this affects your ability to solve problems?

2. If you have a problem to solve, do you usually try to solve it by yourself, or do you ask others for help? If you ask for help, do you ask an adult, a friend, or a brother or sister?

3. What did you learn from this lesson about problem solving that may be useful to you?

Follow-up Activity

Have children work in small groups to develop a skit that would illustrate applying the problem-solving process to a typical fourth-grade problem (for example, fights with friends or being picked last for a team).

Problems & Solutions

PROBLEM-SOLVING STEPS

P   Clearly define the problem.

R   Realistically assess the problem: Is it a big problem or a little problem?

O   Think of all the options.

B   Be aware of consequences.

L   Listen to others' opinions.

E   Eliminate options.

M   Make a problem-solving plan.

the **PASSPORT** PROGRAM

Self-Development
ACTIVITY
1 Wanted: A Kid Like Me
2 My Mistake
3 Me, Not Me
4 Which One Am I?

Emotional Development
ACTIVITY
1 Left Out and Lonely
2 They Can't Make You Feel
3 Why Do I Feel Like This?
4 Ridiculed and Rejected

Social Development
ACTIVITY
1 It Takes Cooperation
2 Fights with Friends
3 Tuning Out Teasing
4 From Their Point of View

Cognitive Development
ACTIVITY
1 It's a Choice
2 Does That Make Sense?
3 Chain Reaction
4 Dubious Decisions

Wanted: A Kid Like Me

Developmental Perspective

A major factor affecting self-development in these school-aged years is peer influence. As children strive to achieve new skills, they are subject not only to their own self-evaluations, but also to feedback from peers. As they become aware of their specific areas of competence, they also may begin to experience a lack of self-confidence, which may affect them in many different ways.

Objective

▷ To identify one's positive attributes

Materials

▷ One envelope of Wanted: A Kid Like Me–Sentence Stems (Handout 1) per child. An alternative would be to make an overhead transparency of Handout 1, asking children to select their characteristics from this list.

▷ Art supplies for each child: pencils, crayons, glue, scissors, construction paper, magazines, yarn, and so forth

▷ A coat hanger and additional art supplies for each child (for the Follow-up Activity)

Procedure

1. Ask children if they have ever seen a "wanted" poster. Usually, the person wanted is a criminal or a missing person. Explain that children are going to be making their own wanted posters, to emphasize their good qualities. Discuss the fact that too often we only think about the things we can't do or don't like about ourselves, and when we think this way, we may not try new things or feel very happy. Stress the idea that nobody is perfect: Everyone has both strengths and weaknesses, but the purpose of this activity is to focus on the positive.

2. Distribute the envelopes of Wanted: A Kid Like Me–Sentence Stems (Handout 1) and the art supplies. Indicate that children are to read the slips of paper in the envelope and select 10 that they want to use to develop a poster. They can use the art supplies in any way they choose, but the end result should be a poster that somehow illustrates the content of the sentence stems they select.

3. Allow time for children to share their wanted posters in small groups, then discuss the Content and Personalization Questions.

Discussion

CONTENT QUESTIONS

1. What did you like or dislike about doing this activity?
2. How did you feel about identifying positive things about yourself to advertise to others?

PERSONALIZATION QUESTIONS

1. Do you think more about what you don't like about yourself than what you do like? If so, why do you think you do this? Is this something you would like to change?
2. If others in your class are better at some things than you are, what does this say about you? Does it take away your positive qualities in other areas?
3. Did you learn anything about yourself from this lesson? If so, what?

Follow-up Activity

Invite children to use the coat hanger and additional art materials to make a mobile of things they like about themselves.

Wanted: A Kid Like Me

SENTENCE STEMS

Leader note: Cut items apart and place in an envelope; give one set to each child.

Something I am really good at is . . .	Something I can do with my brain is . . .
Something I have recently learned to do is . . .	Something I like about my sense of humor is . . .
Something I really like about myself is . . .	Something I like about the way I look is . . .
Something I can do physically (like run fast, jump) is . . .	Three words that would best describe me are . . .
Something positive about the way I get along with others my age is . . .	Something others like about me is . . .
Something positive about the way I get along with adults (parents, teachers) is . . .	Something I do that shows that I am sensitive and kind to people or animals is . . .
Something I think makes me unique or different from others is . . .	Something I like about how I look is . . .
Something I have improved in is . . .	An accomplishment I am proud of is . . .

My Mistake

Developmental Perspective

During this developmental stage, learning and mastery are important tasks. Children need to understand that they will not do everything perfectly and that part of learning is making mistakes. Because they tend to be rather self-critical at this age, it is important to help them see that they are not inadequate or stupid when they don't do everything right.

Objective

▷ To differentiate between making mistakes and being a total failure

Materials

▷ Chalkboard

▷ Paper and pencil for each child

▷ A balloon, a Nerf ball, and a straight pin

Procedure

1. Introduce this lesson by asking children to take out a sheet of paper and number it from 1–5. They are to answer *true* or *false* to the following quiz questions:

    ► Question 1: If a person makes a mistake, it means he or she is stupid.

    ► Question 2: There are people in the world who never make mistakes.

    ► Question 3: Making a mistake is really bad.

    ► Question 4: Grown-ups don't make mistakes.

    ► Question 5: If you make a mistake once, you will just keep on making it.

2. Next write the wrong date and time on the chalkboard. Then call on several children and ask them to share their responses to the quiz. Deliberately call them by the wrong names. Next write the topic for the lesson on the board and spell a word incorrectly.

3. Ask children to help you define the word *mistake*. Ask them what it says about a person if he or she makes a mistake. If they haven't pointed out the mistakes you made, refer to them and discuss them in reference to the quiz questions: Are you stupid because you made mistakes? Was making these mistakes really bad? Does it mean you will keep on making mistakes? Is it natural to make mistakes?

4. Next take the balloon and blow it up. Ask a child to hold the balloon and pretend that he or she is the balloon. Have the child talk about a time he or she made a mistake. As soon as the mistake has been described, pop the balloon. Then ask the child to hold the Nerf ball and talk about the same mistake. As soon as the mistake has been described, poke at the ball with the pin. Explain to children that sometimes when people make mistakes they think they are total failures–that they are "nothing" if they make a mistake. Liken that to the balloon that was destroyed with one mistake. Contrast that to the Nerf ball: A mistake was made, but the ball didn't disappear. There might have been some small holes in it, but that didn't mean the whole ball was destroyed. Explain that this is how it is when people make mistakes: They aren't total failures, and they won't be destroyed when they make one mistake.

5. Ask children to turn their papers over and write about a time they made a mistake and what they learned from making it.

6. Process the activity by asking the Content and Personalization Questions.

Discussion

CONTENT QUESTIONS

1. What does it say about you if you make a mistake?

2. Do you think that most people make mistakes once in a while?

3. Is there a difference between making a mistake and just not trying? How would you explain this difference? Which do you think is worse–to make a mistake or just not try?

PERSONALIZATION QUESTIONS

1. How do you feel when you make mistakes?

2. Do you put yourself down for your mistakes? If so, do you think it is helpful for you to do this? What can you say to yourself so you won't put yourself down the next time you make a mistake?

3. What did you learn from this lesson about making mistakes?

Follow-up Activity

Have children interview their parents or older siblings about a mistake they made and what they learned from it.

Me, Not Me

Developmental Perspective

During this stage of development children are gradually developing a stable and comprehensive self-understanding. Understanding what is "me" and "not me" is an important part of this process.

Objective

▷ To identify specific characteristics that are like or unlike oneself

Materials

▷ Three blank envelopes and a pencil for each child

▷ For each child, an envelope of Me, Not Me–Statements (Handout 2)

Procedure

1. Give each child three blank envelopes and a pencil. First, have children take the blank envelopes and on one of them write *me*, on another write *not me*, and on the third, *sort of like me, sort of not*. Next distribute the envelopes containing the Me, Not Me–Statements (Handout 2). Explain to children that they are to read each of the statements in these envelopes. If they agree with a statement, they should put that slip in the *me* envelope. If they don't agree, they should put it in the *not me* envelope. If the statement is somewhat like them but somewhat not, they should put it in the *sort of like me, sort of not* envelope.

2. After children have sorted their strips, have them share their results with a partner.

3. Process the activity by discussing the Content and Personalization Questions.

Discussion

CONTENT QUESTIONS

1. Was it difficult for you to decide what to put in the envelopes? Were any statements more difficult than others?

2. Were you surprised at some of your responses?

PERSONALIZATION QUESTIONS

1. What did you learn about yourself as a result of this lesson?

2. Do you think how you are on any of these items will change as you get older? (Invite sharing of examples of what might change and why.)

Follow-up Activity

Have children work in groups and make up skits based on their *me, not me,* and *sort of like me, sort of not* characteristics.

Me, Not Me

STATEMENTS

Leader note: Cut items apart and place in an envelope; give each child one set.

I would rather watch television than play outside.	I tend to be shy instead of outgoing in new situations.
I would rather spend time with friends than go somewhere with a parent.	I would rather be taller instead of shorter than my friends.
I would rather go to school than stay home.	I would rather go to church than stay home.
I am better at math than at reading/language arts.	I cheat in order to win a game rather than be honest and lose.
I like dogs better than cats.	I like pizza better than hamburgers.
I like living in the city better than living in the country.	I would tell a lie instead of telling the truth.
I would rather be an only child than have brothers and sisters.	I would rather have a clean room than a messy room.
I would rather play with one friend instead of several.	I think it's better to not take drugs than to take them.
I would rather swim than play basketball.	I think it's better not to smoke than to smoke.
I am better at singing than playing sports.	I am closer to my mom than to my dad.

Which One Am I?

Developmental Perspective

Because rates of development are so varied by the time children reach age 10 or 11, it is not uncommon to see some very sophisticated fifth graders, whereas others are still enjoying the activities characteristic of younger children. Maturational differences can be very confusing and disconcerting as children struggle to figure out who they are.

Objective

▷ To identify feelings associated with varying rates of development

Materials

▷ A pencil and a copy of the Which One Am I? Case Studies (Handout 3) for each child

▷ Several fiction and nonfiction books describing the maturation process (for the Follow-up Activity)

Procedure

1. Introduce this lesson by discussing the fact that people grow at different rates and, as a result, it is not uncommon for some children their age to be content to play the games they did when they were younger, whereas others are more interested in doing things that older kids do. Stress the fact that everyone has a right to be the way he or she is. People don't have to change just because others their age think they should.

2. Distribute the Which One Am I? Case Studies (Handout 3), one per child. Ask children to read them and respond to the questions at the end. Let children know that they will not have to share their answers unless they choose to.

3. To process the activity, ask the Content and Personalization Questions.

Discussion

CONTENT QUESTIONS

1. What did you learn from reading these case studies?

2. Is there anything in these stories that you particularly agree with? Disagree with? (Invite sharing.)

PERSONALIZATION QUESTIONS

1. What do you think is fun about being more grown-up?
2. What do you miss about not being as much of a kid as you used to be?
3. What did you learn from this lesson that applies to you and your life?

Follow-up Activity

Invite children to read fiction and nonfiction books that describe the varying rates in the growing-up process. Examples include *What's Happening to Me? The Answers to Some of the World's Most Embarrassing Questions,* by P. Mayle (Lyle Stuart, 1975), and *It's O.K. to Be You: A Frank and Funny Guide to Growing Up* (Tricycle Press, 1988).

Which One Am I?

CASE STUDIES–PAGE 1

Name: _____ Date: _____

ANNA'S CASE

Anna is almost 11 years old. She still likes to play with dolls and often chooses to spend time with her younger sister and her friend. Together they like to spy on the neighbors, play school, and ride bikes. Lately, however, Anna has been feeling kind of funny about playing with her sister and her friend. She doesn't like to be seen in the neighborhood with them because she's afraid some of the kids in her grade will wonder why she's playing with younger kids. She'd never tell some of the friends in her class that she still likes to play with dolls; she's afraid they'd call her a baby. It all seems rather confusing.

Last week Anna was invited to a sleepover. It was fun at first because they went skating and had pizza. But then several girls started talking about kissing boys, and then they started calling boys on the phone. Anna felt weird–it was like these girls were so much more grown-up than she was. She couldn't imagine kissing a boy–and even though she had some friends that were boys, she didn't think about them the way some of these girls did. She wondered if there was something wrong with her.

Questions

1. Who are you more like? Anna or her friends?

2. Do you still like to do some of the things you did when you were younger?

3. Do you know others your age who still have the same interests you do?

4. Just because some kids your age like to do more grown-up things, or just because some kids your age don't, does this mean you are weird, or does this just mean you are growing up at a different rate than others your age?

Which One Am I?

CASE STUDIES—PAGE 2

TERRELL'S CASE

Terrell and Tyrone lived in the same neighborhood. They had been best friends since kindergarten. Now that they were almost 11, though, they were not spending as much time together. To begin with, one day when they were walking home from school, Tyrone offered Terrell a cigarette. Terrell was shocked . . . he didn't know that Tyrone ever did anything like that. At first he said no, but Tyrone said, "What are you, some kind of baby?" So Terrell took one.

The next time Terrell asked Tyrone if he wanted to ride bikes or play sandlot baseball, Tyrone laughed at him and said those things were for little kids; he'd rather hang out in the mall at the arcade. Terrell felt really bad. They had been friends a long time, but it was as though they didn't have much in common anymore. Tyrone was acting a lot more grown-up than Terrell felt.

Questions

1. Which one are you more like? Tyrone or Terrell?

2. Do you still like to do some of the things you did when you were younger?

3. Do you know others your age who still have the same interests you do?

4. Just because some kids your age like to do more grown-up things, or just because some kids your age don't, does this mean you are weird, or does this just mean that you are growing up at a different rate than others your age?

Left Out & Lonely

Developmental Perspective

As children enter the latter part of middle childhood, peer acceptance becomes more important to them. Related to this is the fear of being left out or not being chosen (or chosen last) for a team. Oftentimes children are hesitant or unable to express verbally how they are feeling and therefore assume that they are the only ones who feel left out and lonely. It is important to help children learn that they are not the only ones who feel this way and to give them some tools to handle these emotions.

Objectives

▷ To learn that others experience rejection and feel lonely

▷ To learn effective ways to deal with rejection and loneliness

Materials

▷ A copy of the Left Out and Lonely–Worksheet (Handout 4) and a pencil for each child

Procedure

1. Distribute the Left Out and Lonely–Worksheets (Handout 4), one per child. Explain to children that they will be participating in a Left Out and Lonely Hunt, where the objective is to see if they can find others who have experienced the same situations listed on the worksheet.

2. Once children have their worksheets completed (or after a period of time that has allowed most of them to get the signatures), process the activity by discussing the Content and Personalization Questions.

Discussion

CONTENT QUESTIONS

1. Was it difficult for you to find people to sign your sheets?

2. Were you surprised that so many other people have felt left out and lonely?

PERSONALIZATION QUESTIONS

1. Have you ever felt left out and lonely? If so, what has that been like for you?

2. Have you ever included anyone in one of your activities when that person was left out? Has anyone ever included you?

3. What do you do to help yourself deal with your feelings when you feel lonely because you have been left out?

4. If you are left out, does it mean that no one likes you? What does it mean?

Follow-up Activity

Ask children to think about inviting someone who looks lonely or has been left out to join them in an activity.

Left Out & Lonely

WORKSHEET

Name: _____ Date: _____

Instructions: Write your name and the date at the top of the worksheet. Next walk around the group and ask others if they have ever experienced any of the situations listed. If so, ask them to sign their name on one of the lines provided. No single person can sign more than two spaces on your sheet. When all of your spaces have been signed, take your seat.

Name

1. Has been picked last for a team sport.

   _____

2. Has not been invited to a friend's birthday party.

   _____

3. Has not been asked to stay overnight with a friend.

   _____

4. Has not been picked to be on a team at recess.

   _____

5. Has been left out of a group activity in the classroom.

   _____

6. Didn't get to go on a family outing when a brother or sister did.

   _____

7. Didn't get asked to sit by your best friend at lunch.

   _____

8. Got picked last for a spelling contest.

   _____

9. Didn't get selected to be the class helper.

   _____

10. Got left out of a kickball game.

    _____

They Can't Make You Feel

Developmental Perspective

Although children at this age are beginning to realize that they are not the direct cause of another person's emotional discomfort, it is still very natural for them to think that something or someone "made" them feel a certain way. Children begin to experience more negative emotions as they deal with mastery in academic tasks, peer relations, and competition in team sports, clubs, or other activities. It is therefore important to help them understand that they do have some emotional control.

Objectives

▷ To learn that nobody "makes" you feel the way you do

▷ To understand the connection between thoughts and feelings

Materials

▷ A copy of the They Can't Make You Feel–Scenarios (Handout 5) and a pencil for each child

▷ A copy of They Can't Make You Feel–Worksheet (Handout 6) for each partnership

Procedure

1. Introduce the lesson by asking children if they think people always feel the same way about the same situation. If they agree that everyone doesn't always feel the same way, ask them what they think accounts for the differences, bringing out the fact that the way we think about things influences our feelings. For example, if you live in a climate where it hardly ever snows, you might be excited if you hear that a snowstorm is brewing because you don't very often get to go sledding or skiing. However, if you live in a climate where it snows a lot, you might be sick of snow and tired of sledding and skiing, so you would be disappointed to hear that a storm is coming.

2. Give a copy of the They Can't Make You Feel–Scenarios (Handout 5) to each child. Ask children to read the scenarios and identify both their thoughts and their feelings on the blank lines. When they are finished, have them discuss their thoughts and feelings with a partner.

3. After they have finished sharing with their partners, discuss the Content Questions with the group.

4. After discussing the Content Questions, distribute a copy of the They Can't Make You Feel–Worksheet (Handout 6) to each partnership. Have the partners answer the questions at the end of Part 1. Review partners' answers to questions and summarize the main concept as follows:

> In real life, how you think about a situation does affect the way you feel about it. If you tell yourself that it is awful and terrible and that you can't stand it, you will probably feel very angry, upset, or frustrated. However, if you tell yourself that you don't like it but it isn't the end of the world and you don't have to pay attention to it or get upset about it, you will feel disappointed or a little upset, but you won't be super upset or angry.

5. Have partners complete Part 2: Each thinks of a situation in which he or she has experienced angry or upset feelings. After they briefly describe these situations, they work together to see if they can change their feelings by thinking differently, using the examples in Part 1 of the worksheet to help them do this.

6. Allow time for partners to share their ideas and discuss the process, then discuss the Personalization Questions.

Discussion

CONTENT QUESTIONS

1. Did you and your partner agree on the feelings for each scenario? If you didn't, why do you think you didn't?

2. How would you like it if someone told you that the first situation always *makes* kids feel mad? Do you think that is true?

3. Do you think that people or situations *make* you feel the way you do, or do you have a choice?

4. What is the connection between your thoughts and your feelings?

PERSONALIZATION QUESTIONS

1. Have you ever said something like this: "She made me so mad" or "That really made me feel hurt"?

2. Do you really think someone else can *make* you mad or hurt, or do you make yourself feel that way? If you think you make yourself feel that way, how does that happen?

3. What can you remember from this lesson that will help you in the future when you have problems with your feelings?

Follow-up Activity

Invite children to listen to their language. Each time they catch themselves saying things like "She made me feel . . ." or "They made me so angry," have them change their language to "I felt angry about . . ." They can also politely challenge others on this point so everyone becomes more aware that others don't actually make us feel anything.

They Can't Make You Feel

SCENARIOS—PAGE 1

Name: _____ Date: _____

Instructions: Read each of the following scenarios. First try to identify what you think about this situation. For example, if you think older kids shouldn't be able to tell you what to do, you might be upset or mad about the first scenario, but if you have other things to do and don't particularly care if you play or not, you might just feel so-so—it might not be a big deal. After you have identified your thoughts, write how you would feel in the blank space.

1. You are playing kickball in the neighborhood. One of the older kids comes up to you and says that you can't play.

   You think: _____

   You feel: _____

2. You are at the grocery store with your mom. You want her to buy you some candy, and she says she barely has enough money for milk and cereal.

   You think: _____

   You feel: _____

3. Your class is going to perform in the school assembly. The teacher tells you to dress up in your very best clothes and your good shoes. You don't have any very nice clothes and you only have one pair of shoes.

   You think: _____

   You feel: _____

4. Your dad got in trouble with the law and has to go to jail. Kids at school find out and start teasing you about it.

   You think: _____

   You feel: _____

5. You are out for lunch recess. You want to play basketball, but there are already too many kids playing.

   You think: _____

   You feel: _____

They Can't Make You Feel

SCENARIOS–PAGE 2

6. Two of your friends are sitting by themselves in the lunchroom. They look over at you and start giggling and whispering.

   You think: _____

   You feel: _____

7. You just got your hair cut last night. You really like it. Today kids are teasing you about how bad you look.

   You think: _____

   You feel: _____

8. Someone in your class asks you to go rollerblading on Saturday, but your stepmother says you can't go.

   You think: _____

   You feel: _____

9. Some kids in your neighborhood are going on a picnic. They don't invite you to go along.

   You think: _____

   You feel: _____

10. Your little brother comes into your room when you are gone and takes one of your computer games so he can play it.

    You think: _____

    You feel: _____

They Can't Make You Feel

WORKSHEET–PAGE 1

PART 1

Instructions: Read and discuss the two following situations, then answer the questions with your partner.

Sheniqua and Shantel

Sheniqua and Shantel are standing in the lunch line. The two girls ahead of them keep turning around and looking at them, then start giggling and whispering.

Suppose you are Sheniqua. You:

- ► See the two girls looking at you.

- ► Hear them giggling and whispering.

- ► Think to yourself: "They are giggling and whispering about us, and that is awful. They shouldn't make fun of us."

- ► You feel . . . angry.

Now suppose you are Shantel. You:

- ► See the two girls looking at you.

- ► Hear them giggling and whispering.

- ► Think to yourself: "They are giggling and whispering about us. I don't like it, but I don't have to pay attention to it."

- ► You feel . . . a little irritated.

They Can't Make You Feel

WORKSHEET-PAGE 2

Tyler and Thomas

Tyler and Thomas are playing Nintendo. Their older brother comes in and starts yelling at them to get washed up for supper.

Suppose you are Tyler. You:

- ► See your brother walk into the room.

- ► Hear him yell at you.

- ► Think to yourself: "He has no right to yell at us. He is always so mean. I can't stand the way he acts."

- ► You feel . . . angry.

Now suppose you are Thomas. You:

- ► See your brother walk into the room.

- ► Hear him yell at you.

- ► Think to yourself: "I hate it when he does this. He yells too much. I don't know why he can't just ask us to get washed up instead of yelling."

- ► You feel . . . irritated.

Questions

1. Why do you think the two girls felt differently about the same situation?

2. Why do you think the two boys felt differently about the same situation?

3. Do you think this happened to you and your partner in the They Can't Make You Feel–Scenarios? If you and your partner felt differently about some of the scenarios, go back and discuss your thoughts and see if your feelings change if your thoughts change.

They Can't Make You Feel

WORKSHEET–PAGE 3

PART 2

Instructions: Think of a situation (one per partner) in which you have experienced angry or upset feelings. Write these situations below. Then work together to see if you can change your feelings by thinking differently. Use the examples from Part 1 to help you.

Partner 1

My situation: _____

_____

_____

_____

_____

Partner 2

My situation: _____

_____

_____

_____

_____

Why Do I Feel Like This?

Developmental Perspective

Despite the fact that middle childhood has been described as one of the easiest developmental periods, many children live in dysfunctional family situations. These children must contend with more than just the normal experiences and stressors of this period. Many children struggle with uncomfortable feelings in conjunction with these situations. It is important to help them learn to identify, express, and deal effectively with these feelings.

Objectives

▷ To identify commonly experienced uncomfortable emotions

▷ To learn effective ways to deal with uncomfortable emotions

Materials

▷ One Why Do I Feel Like This? Game Board (Handout 7) and one Why Do I Feel Like This? Situations Sheet (Handout 8) for every four children

▷ One game token and one penny for every two children

Procedure

1. Divide children into teams of four and distribute the Why Do I Feel Like This? Game Boards (Handout 7) and Situations Sheets (Handout 8). Within each group of four, give each pair of partners a game token and a penny.

2. Explain the game's procedures: As a team, children read the first situation, talk about how they would feel, and then select one of the ways to deal with the situation (or come up with their own idea). Then one member of each partnership flips a coin to determine how many spaces the partners can move (heads = 2 spaces, tails = 1 space).

3. Have children continue playing the game until all situations have been read or one set of partners reaches the end of the game board.

4. To process the activity, discuss the Content and Personalization Questions.

Discussion

CONTENT QUESTIONS

1. Which feeling did you identify most frequently?

2. Were there some situations where you could have had more than one feeling? (Invite sharing of examples.)

3. Was it difficult to think about how you would deal with these feelings? Were some situations more difficult than others? (Share examples.)

PERSONALIZATION QUESTIONS

1. Have you or someone you know had some of these same experiences? (Invite sharing.)

2. Have you ever experienced feelings similar to the ones you identified in these situations?

3. How do you, or someone you know, handle family situations in which you feel angry, worried, scared, or embarrassed?

4. Do you think that if you changed your thoughts, this would also help the way you feel? For example, if your dad was supposed to pick you up for the weekend and never showed up, you might feel very sad if you think your dad might not love you because he didn't show up. If you change your thought to "Just because he didn't show up doesn't mean he doesn't love me," you might not be as sad. (Invite children to share examples of how they could use this process.)

Follow-up Activity

Read a story to children illustrating positive ways of coping with adverse family situations. Good stories to try are *Living with a Single Parent,* by M. Rosenberg (Bradbury Press, 1992), and *A Birthday Present for Daniel: A Child's Story of Loss,* by J. Rothman (Prometheus Books, 1996).

Why Do I Feel Like This?

GAME BOARD

Instructions: As a group, look at the first situation on the Why Do I Feel Like This? Situations Sheet. Discuss how you would feel about this situation and how you would handle it, either by selecting one of the options given or by coming up with your own solution. Have one member of each partnership flip the coin to see how many spaces the partners can move (heads = 2 spaces, tails = 1 space). Continue playing until all the situations have been read or one of the partnerships reaches the end of the game board.

Why Do I Feel Like This?

SITUATIONS SHEET–PAGE 1

1. Your parents are yelling and fighting again. You feel _____ and you . . .
   ► Stay in your room and try to concentrate on something else.
   ► Get in the middle and beg them to stop fighting.
   ► Tell yourself it is their problem.
   ► (Your solution.) _____
   _____

2. Your family doesn't have much money, and you have been delivering papers so you could buy your own bike. You finally have enough money to buy the one you want. Your grandmother is going to pick you up after school to go to the store, so you take your money to school. When you look in your desk at the end of the day it is gone. You feel _____ and you . . .
   ► Ask the teacher to ask the class who took the money.
   ► Pretend that it's no big deal.
   ► Approach the person you think took it.
   ► (Your solution.) _____
   _____

3. You have to walk by the local bar on the way home from school. You see your dad's car and know that he must be inside drinking. You feel _____ and you . . .
   ► Go to the door and ask him to go home with you.
   ► Walk on home and get busy so you won't think about it.
   ► Tell yourself that you can't change him.
   ► (Your solution.) _____
   _____

4. You made a new friend at school, and you invite her to spend the night. When she comes your brother won't leave you alone. Your parents continually yell at you to play with him and tell you that if you don't, your friend has to leave. You feel _____ and you . . .
   ► Apologize to your friend that this is happening.
   ► Just pretend that nothing is bothering you.
   ► Talk to your friend about the problems in your family.
   ► (Your solution.) _____
   _____

Why Do I Feel Like This?

SITUATIONS SHEET–PAGE 2

5. Your parents are divorced. You don't see your mom very often, but she has promised to take you out to eat for your birthday. On the day she is supposed to come, you stand by the window and wait, but she doesn't show up. You call her apartment, and there is no answer. You feel _____ and you . . .

   ▶ Go to your room and cry.

   ▶ Call a friend and go outside to play so you can get your mind on something else.

   ▶ Think to yourself that your mom loves you even if she doesn't act like she does.

   ▶ (Your solution.) _____
   _____

6. Your dad just lost his job, and there isn't much money to buy new clothes. Your mother bought some things at a garage sale, and some of the kids at school have been teasing you about how you look. You feel _____ and you . . .

   ▶ Try to ignore them.

   ▶ Tease them about how they look.

   ▶ Just tell yourself that you look nice no matter what they say.

   ▶ (Your solution.) _____
   _____

7. Your mother just got remarried, and you have moved into your stepfather's house with his two sons. You caught one of the sons smoking behind the house, and he threatened to beat you up if you told his dad. You feel _____ and you . . .

   ▶ Tell your mom and ask her for help.

   ▶ Pretend you didn't see anything.

   ▶ Tell your stepfather.

   ▶ (Your solution.) _____
   _____

8. School has just started, and the teacher is asking students to share where they went on summer vacation. Your parents couldn't afford a vacation, so the only place you went was to the park. You feel _____ and you . . .

   ▶ Make up a story about where you went.

   ▶ Tell the truth.

   ▶ Just say that you don't feel like sharing.

   ▶ (Your solution.) _____
   _____

Why Do I Feel Like This?

SITUATIONS SHEET–PAGE 3

9. You forgot to make your bed and pick up your room. Your stepmother starts yelling at you, saying that you never do anything right and that she and your dad would be happier if you would go live with your mother. You feel _____ and you . . .

   ▶ Get mad at her and tell her she's wrong.

   ▶ Tell your dad what she said.

   ▶ Just do what she wants you to do.

   ▶ (Your solution.) _____

   _____

10. Your older brother got caught stealing a car and driving after he had been drinking. He has to spend time in jail. You feel _____ and you . . .

    ▶ Go to visit him whenever you can.

    ▶ Act like he's not part of your family.

    ▶ Tell yourself that he is still your brother and you can still care about him even if his behavior was bad.

    ▶ (Your solution.) _____

    _____

11. Your mother has a new boyfriend. He always comes to your room and wants to kiss you goodnight. You don't know him very well, and he never comes in with your mother. You feel _____ and you . . .

    ▶ Tell your mom what is happening.

    ▶ Tell him to leave you alone.

    ▶ Just let him kiss you.

    ▶ (Your solution.) _____

    _____

12. Your mom comes home late from work, and you think she has been drinking. You hurry around and try to start supper and take care of your sister because you don't want your dad to be mad when he comes home. You feel _____ and you . . .

    ▶ Beg your mom to stop drinking before your dad gets home.

    ▶ Just get supper and pretend that nothing is wrong.

    ▶ Recognize that you can't stop your mom from drinking.

    ▶ (Your solution.) _____

    _____

Ridiculed & Rejected

Developmental Perspective

Children at this age are becoming more involved with peer relations, but with that involvement comes fear of rejection and ridicule. It is important to help children see that many other children have these same fears and to look at ways to deal with their feelings.

Objective

▷ To learn effective ways to deal with ridicule and rejection

Materials

▷ A copy of the Ridiculed and Rejected–Story (Handout 9) for each child

▷ A pencil and sheet of paper for each child (for the Follow-up Activity)

Procedure

1. Ask children to raise their hands if the following situations have ever happened to them:

   ► Someone has made fun of the way you look.

   ► Someone has made fun of the way you walk, run, throw, or catch.

   ► Someone has told you that he or she never wants to be your friend.

   ► Someone has told you that he or she doesn't like you.

   ► Someone has told you that you're ugly or you smell.

2. Discuss with children the fact that many of them have experienced rejection or ridicule from others. Ask children to identify words that describe how they feel when this occurs.

3. Read the Ridiculed and Rejected–Story (Handout 9), or have children read the story to themselves.

4. After the story, discuss the Content and Personalization Questions.

Discussion

CONTENT QUESTIONS

1. Who felt ridiculed and rejected in this story?

2. What helped Maria when she had been treated this way?

3. Why do you think Carolina said these things to Marta?

4. What did you think about the way Maria treated Marta? About how Carolina treated Marta?

PERSONALIZATION QUESTIONS

1. Has anyone ever treated you the way Maria and Marta were treated? If so, how did you feel?

2. Have you ever treated anyone the way Carolina treated Marta? If so, why do you suppose you did that, and how did you feel about it?

3. If you have been ridiculed or rejected, how did you deal with your feelings?

4. Do you think any of the ideas Maria shared with Marta would work for you? What else could you do to deal with your feelings if you have been ridiculed or rejected?

Follow-up Activity

Have children write an advice column for a make-believe local paper, sharing ideas about how to deal with ridicule and rejection.

Ridiculed & Rejected

STORY–PAGE 1

Maria, a fifth grader, was eating lunch with Marta, a fourth grader. They were just about finished when Carolina walked over to the table. "Maria, why are you eating with this creep?" she asked, looking at Marta. "Don't you know that she lies and cheats? Why do you want to sit by her when you can have better friends? Besides that, she's just a fourth grader. Why are you hanging out with babies?"

Maria was shocked that Carolina would say something like that. She glanced over at Marta and noticed tears in her eyes. Maria didn't know what to do or say. She hadn't known Marta very long, but she was her partner in reading workshop, which met right before lunch, so they had gotten into the habit of walking to the lunchroom together after the class. Maria had never seen Marta cheat, and she had no reason to think she lied. She didn't know why Carolina would say those things about her.

Maria knew what it felt like to be in Marta's situation, though. Last year something similar had happened to her. Maria hadn't done anything wrong that she could think of, but all of a sudden one of her classmates had started calling her names and told her that she couldn't be in the after-school treehouse club that met in the neighborhood. When Maria told her mother about it, her mother said that things like this sometimes happen in fourth, fifth, and sixth grades because nobody thinks about how the other person might feel before they say things. She explained to Maria that sometimes kids this age get jealous of each other, which means that maybe they are afraid someone is more popular or has nicer clothes or is smarter or better liked by the teacher. So to make themselves feel better, they try to hurt someone else by rejecting or ridiculing them. Maria's mother told her that just because someone does that to you doesn't mean you should do it back and that you have to stop and ask yourself if what the people are saying about you is true. If it isn't, then you have to remember that "sticks and stones can break your bones, but words can never hurt you–unless you let them."

Ridiculed & Rejected

STORY—PAGE 2

Maria understood what her mother had told her, but she had still been upset. She didn't understand why someone would do this to her, because she wasn't trying to show off or act hot or anything. She didn't say bad things about people, so she didn't understand why they would do that either. Maria had been so sad and confused about this that she had gone to see the school counselor. The counselor had listened to what had happened and had asked Maria to put one of her hands out flat on the table. The counselor then had Maria hold up each finger and identify something she liked (or others liked about her). After she had listed five things, the counselor had her tighten her hand into a fist and hold it in front of her. She explained to Maria that these were her good qualities and that no one could take them away. No matter how many kids ridiculed or rejected her, that didn't take away from her good qualities. She suggested to Maria that the next time this happened to her, she should remember her list and hold up her fist to remind her that she had good qualities, even if some people didn't think so. The counselor had also explained to her that kids this age are sometimes very cruel, and while we might not be able to control them, we would only make the situation worse if we did the same thing back to them. She had told Maria that in time the situation would probably take care of itself but that if it continued, then something more would have to be done. The counselor asked Maria what she thought she could do in the meantime to help herself feel less upset. Maria told her that she was going to think about all the people who did like her and said good things about her rather than thinking about the ones who were mean.

So as Maria sat with her new friend, she remembered what it had been like for her last year. She told Marta what the counselor had said, thinking that this might help Marta. She also told Marta that the more she thought about it, the more unhappy she would be, so she suggested that they go out for recess and find something to do. If the other girls didn't want to play with them, that was just too bad. They would find something else to do and not sit around and mope about it.

It Takes Cooperation

Developmental Perspective

As children become more social, they may join organizations such as scouts, participate on sports teams, or attend camps or club activities. As a result, their need to develop cooperative behaviors increases. Specific instruction in children's roles as part of a group can facilitate their social development.

Objectives

▷ To identify cooperative behaviors

▷ To practice cooperative behaviors

Materials

▷ Three Ping-Pong balls and a small bucket or plastic container for each team of 5–6 children

▷ A spoon for each team member

▷ A long strip of masking tape placed across one end of the room

Procedure

1. Assign children to teams of 5–6 members and distribute three Ping-Pong balls and a small bucket or plastic container to each team. Give each team member a spoon.

2. Instruct each team that their task is to move their three Ping-Pong balls to the bucket at the end of the room, one ball at a time. To do this, each player must place one hand behind his or her back and pass the ball to the spoon of the next team member. If the ball is dropped, team members must discuss what to do and work together to get the ball back on the spoon. To get the ball on the spoon, they must use their spoons and only one hand per individual. Team members are to continue passing the ball until it reaches the last team member, who descends to his or her knees, then drops the ball from the spoon into the bucket.

3. Process the activity by discussing the Content and Personalization Questions.

Discussion

Content Questions

1. How did you and your team members cooperate in order to move the Ping-Pong balls to the bucket?

2. Were there any examples of uncooperative behavior? If so, how do you think this affected the process?

3. What are some examples of other cooperative behaviors that you didn't use in this activity but would be helpful to you in future activities?

PERSONALIZATION QUESTIONS

1. Do you think you are generally someone who cooperates well?

2. Which cooperative behaviors do you use the most?

3. Have you been in situations where other children haven't been cooperative? If so, how did you feel about this? Do you like to work or play with people who don't cooperate?

4. What would you like to continue doing (or change) relative to your cooperative behavior?

Follow-up Activity

Invite children to invent games in which they would need to cooperate to complete a task. Provide time for them to present their games to others and to involve others in the cooperative process.

Fights with Friends

Developmental Perspective

In the latter part of middle childhood, children have a broader repertoire of social skills. Despite this, children continue to exclude others and can be cruel about teasing. Conflicts readily develop because there is more pressure from peers to engage in inappropriate activities, and children's need to excel can sometimes result in unhealthy competition. Fights with friends are common and a major source of frustration.

Objective

▷ To learn effective conflict management skills

Materials

▷ Chalkboard

▷ One copy of the Fights with Friends–Problem-Solving Wheel (Handout 10) and a pencil for each child

▷ A set of Fights with Friends–Conflict Cards (Handout 11) for each group of three children

Procedure

1. Introduce the lesson by asking children to think about the last argument, conflict, or fight they had with a friend. Without using names of others, invite discussion about the types of conflicts and how children resolved them.

2. Divide children into groups of three. Distribute the Fights with Friends–Problem-Solving Wheel (Handout 10) to each child and a set of Fights with Friends–Conflict Cards (Handout 11) to each group. Instruct children to take turns drawing a conflict card and reading it aloud. As a group, they should brainstorm ways to handle the conflict. The child who drew the card fills in the "spokes" of his or her own conflict wheel with the alternatives discussed. Next have children identify the positive and negative aspects of each alternative. The child who drew the card puts an asterisk (*) beside the alternative he or she feels would be the best way to handle the conflict.

3. Continue with this procedure by having another child draw a conflict card, discuss options with the group, fill in the spokes of the wheel, and select the best alternative after considering the positive and negative aspects of each.

4. Process the activity by discussing the Content and Personalization Questions.

Discussion

CONTENT QUESTIONS

1. Were some conflicts more difficult to identify alternatives for than others? (Invite sharing of specific situations.)

2. As a group, were you able to identify what you considered to be good alternatives? (Ask for examples and list on the chalkboard. As the alternatives are stated, ask children to evaluate them as being good, fair, or poor ways of resolving conflict.)

3. What do you think prevents some children from selecting better ways to resolve their conflicts?

PERSONALIZATION QUESTIONS

1. When you have conflicts with friends, do you use some of the alternatives you identified? (Invite children to share examples.)

2. When you and your friends fight, what sorts of things do you fight about? How do you feel when you fight?

3. What are some things you can say to yourself or do to avoid fighting with friends?

Follow-up Activity

Invite children to select three of the strategies identified in this lesson to try when they have conflicts with friends. Suggest that they write a short report about the success or failure of these strategies.

Fights with Friends

PROBLEM-SOLVING WHEEL

Name: _____ Date: _____

Instructions: Take turns drawing a Fights with Friends–Conflict Card, reading it aloud, and brainstorming with other group members ways to handle the conflict. The person who draws the card fills in the "spokes" of his or her conflict wheel with the ideas group members identify, discusses the positive and negative aspects of each idea, then puts an asterisk (*) beside the idea he or she thinks is best.

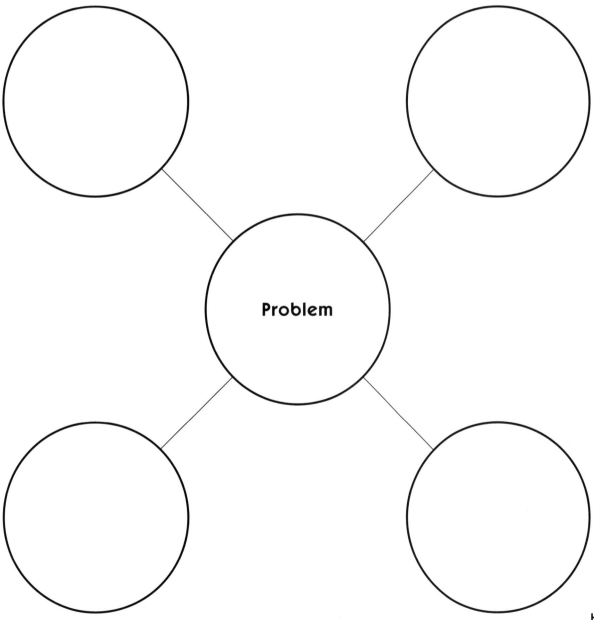

Fights with Friends

CONFLICT CARDS

Leader note: Cut apart; give one set of cards to each group of three children.

A good friend ignores you at lunch recess.

One of your math partners calls you stupid.

Someone likes a boy you like.
(For boys: Someone likes a girl you like.)

Your friend says she doesn't want to play with you after school.

A classmate says bad things about your mother.

Two friends are having a party, and they invite everyone in the class except you.

Two of your friends are whispering and looking at you.

You and your friend start arguing about rules to a game.

The kid who sits behind you keeps kicking your chair.

You and your friend can't agree on where to ride your bikes.

Kids you are playing kickball with call you a cheater.

(Make up your own.)

Tuning Out Teasing

Developmental Perspective

During this period of development, when peer relationships are so important, it is not uncommon for children to feel devastated when they are excluded, teased, or put down. And because they still think very concretely, they do not readily see that there are alternative ways of thinking, feeling, and behaving in these situations. Achieving a broader perspective is an important aspect of children's social development.

Objectives

▷ To identify personal behaviors that may result in exclusion, teasing, or put-downs

▷ To identify a variety of ways to think, feel, and behave when being excluded, teased, or put down

▷ To recognize how controlling one's thinking affects the way one feels and behaves in conflict situations

Materials

▷ A copy of the Tuning Out Teasing–Worksheet (Handout 12) for each partnership

▷ Paper and a pencil for each child

Procedure

1. Introduce the lesson by asking children to take out paper and pencil and identify the following:

   ▶ A time they have been excluded, teased, or put down by peers

   ▶ How they felt about this

   ▶ How they handled the situation

   ▶ Whether they behaved in a way that could have influenced others to react that way to them (did they call them names first, tease them, and so on)

2. Discuss several examples children identify, including feelings and what children did in the situation. Then talk about behaviors that may influence others' reactions. For example, if they call someone a name, they shouldn't be too surprised if someone does this back to them. Encourage discussion about what children can and cannot control in relationships with others: They can control their own behavior (so they don't have to initiate anything or even respond to what others do or say), but they can't necessarily control what others choose to do.

3. Ask children to find a partner and give each partnership a Tuning Out Teasing–Worksheet (Handout 12). Ask partners to read these situations and identify responses.

4. Discuss responses to the worksheet by first identifying any "trigger" behaviors that may have caused the reactions. Then discuss whether children are in control of their own behavior and whether they have to respond to the trigger behaviors of others. Use the following explanation as a way of illustrating how children can control their own behavior, even if they can't control what others say or do:

> Whenever someone does something that you feel angry about or irritated and upset with, you have choices. You can react to it, which often triggers another reaction from the person, or you can deal with it yourself. For example, suppose someone comes up to you and calls you a name. You could get angry and retaliate in some manner, or you could use *self-talk*. You could say to yourself: "Am I what they say I am? And even if I am, does it mean I'm no good? What good is it going to do me to get upset? What good will it do me to punch him or her? What are my other options?" By thinking things through in this way you can see that you don't have to be upset. That doesn't mean you will like it when people tease you, put you down, or exclude you. But you don't have to act out in ways that could make the situation worse.

5. Ask partners to refer again to the Tuning Out Teasing–Worksheet. Have them take two of the examples and identify what the children could have said to themselves so they wouldn't be as upset by something someone else said or did. Allow partners time to share with the total group.

6. To process the activity, discuss the Content and Personalization Questions.

Discussion

CONTENT QUESTIONS

1. Do you think you can usually control how others treat you? Are there some times when your behavior may influence others to act as they do? If so, are you in control of what you do?

2. Do you have to believe what others may say about you if they tease you or put you down?

PERSONALIZATION QUESTIONS

1. Do you usually get upset or angry if someone puts you down, teases you, or excludes you?

2. How do you think self-talk might help you to handle these kinds of situations?

3. Is there anything about your behavior that needs to be changed so there is less chance it will trigger a reaction in others? If so, what is this, and how will you change it?

Follow-up Activity

Divide students into small groups and have them make up skits to illustrate the points covered in this lesson.

Tuning Out Teasing

WORKSHEET–PAGE 1

Instructions: Read each of the situations. Discuss them with your partner, then fill in the blanks.

SITUATION 1

Tanya is standing by herself on the playground. Two girls walk past and say, in snotty voices, that they don't want her anywhere near them because she's poor and her dad drinks.

Questions

1. Did Tanya do anything that could have influenced the girls to act like this? _____

   If so, what did she do?_____

2. Can Tanya control what these girls say to her? _____

   If so, how? _____

3. Can Tanya control how she reacts to the girls? _____

   If so, how? _____

SITUATION 2

Kareem finished his math paper, and the teacher said he had gotten the problems all right. His partner was still working on hers. Kareem went back to his table and said, "Ha, ha. I finished before you did, and I still got them all right." His partner said, "Big deal. Last time you got a really bad grade, so you're not as hot as you think."

Questions

1. Did Kareem do anything that could have influenced his partner to act like this?_____

   If so, what did he do? _____

2. Can Kareem's partner control what Kareem says to her?_____

   If so, how? _____

3. Can Kareem control what he does? _____

   If so, how? _____

Tuning Out Teasing

WORKSHEET–PAGE 2

SITUATION 3

Philip was watching television, and his older brother came up
and started picking on him. Philip lost his temper and punched
his brother.

Questions

1. Did Philip's brother do anything that could have influenced Philip to act like this? _____

   If so, what did he do? _____

2. Can Philip control what his brother does? _____

   If so, how? _____

3. Can Philip control what he does? If so, how?_____

SITUATION 4

Shiron was standing in line for the drinking fountain, and Matt came up
and pushed him out of the way, saying that stupid people have to go to
the back of the line.

Questions

1. Did Shiron do anything that could have influenced Matt to act like this? _____

   If so, what did he do? _____

2. Can Shiron control what Matt does?_____

   If so, how? _____

3. Can Shiron control what he does? _____

   If so, how? _____

From Their Point of View

Developmental Perspective

Although children at this age are less egocentric than before and have the ability, for the most part, to see the world from another's perspective, they often fail to apply this skill consistently. As a result, misunderstandings with parents, teachers, and peers are not uncommon. Reinforcing skills in perspective taking can enhance interpersonal relationships.

Objective

▷ To develop the ability to see things from another's perspective

Materials

▷ A copy of the From Their Point of View–Worksheet (Handout 13) and a pencil for each child

▷ A pair of old glasses, with a pair of yellow and a pair of blue construction paper shapes that can be taped over the lenses

Procedure

1. Introduce the lesson by asking for two volunteers. In private, instruct these volunteers that you will be reading a short scenario. After you have finished reading, you will give one of them the pair of glasses (with yellow lenses). That volunteer will talk aloud to him- or herself as if everything about the situation is wonderful–things will turn out fine, nothing will be a problem, and so on. Share an example: If the scenario reads that there is a hard test tomorrow, the child with the yellow lenses will say, "I'm sure I will do fine. It is probably easy. Even if I don't do fine, I won't worry about it and things will just be wonderful." Then explain that after the first volunteer has shared, you will read the same scenario again. This time you will give the glasses (with blue lenses) to the second volunteer. This volunteer's monologue will be gloomy, sad, terrible, bad, and so on: "I'll flunk because I'm so stupid. Nothing I do is ever right. Everything is just terrible."

2. Explain to the rest of the children that you will be reading a situation that the two volunteers will react to. Children are to listen carefully to see how the perspective changes, based on the color of lenses in the glasses the volunteers are wearing.

3. Read the following scenario to Volunteer 1, who will be wearing the glasses with the yellow lenses:

    > My mom is going out of town, and she is taking me to stay with my aunt. My aunt doesn't have any kids my age, and she lives in the country. I will be there three days with my little baby cousins.

    After Volunteer 1 responds with his or her monologue, put the blue lenses on the glasses and hand them to Volunteer 2, who will respond from the opposite perspective.

4. After the demonstration, discuss the differences between the two viewpoints and introduce the idea of *perspective taking,* or seeing something from another's point of view. In the example, two people "saw" the same situation very differently. Ask children if they think this ever happens among people and elicit some examples. For instance, you think you should get to stay up late because tomorrow is Saturday, but your parents think you should go to bed at your usual bedtime so you won't be crabby.

5. Distribute a copy of the From Their Point of View–Worksheet (Handout 13) to each child. Have each child find a partner and work together to identify the two different perspectives.

6. When partners have finished, allow some time for sharing responses with the total group, then discuss the Content and Personalization Questions.

Discussion

CONTENT QUESTIONS

1. What does taking another perspective or considering another point of view mean?

2. Why do you think people sometimes have different perspectives or points of view about the same situation? (Emphasize that how people think about the situation determines the perspectives they take.)

3. Did you have difficulty identifying the different points of view as you and your partner completed the worksheet?

4. How do you think your relationships with others would be improved if you were better able to see their perspectives?

PERSONALIZATION QUESTIONS

1. Have you ever had difficulty getting along with someone because the two of you had very different perspectives about the same situation? If so, how did you resolve the problem?

2. How do you think you will apply what you have learned in this lesson to your interactions with friends? With parents? With teachers?

Follow-up Activity

Have children select a favorite television show to watch. Encourage them to see if they can identify different perspectives of the characters involved.

From Their Point of View

WORKSHEET–PAGE 1

Instructions: Read each of the situations with your partner, then decide which person's point of view you will each take. Each partner writes what he or she thinks that person's point of view is. When you have both finished writing, discuss your two points of view.

1. Sara is having trouble in math. Her father wants her to get a tutor, but Sara doesn't like this idea.

   Sara's point of view: _____

   _____

   Her father's point of view: _____

   _____

2. Allison and Emily are fighting because Allison didn't sit by Emily at the assembly.

   Allison's point of view:_____

   _____

   Emily's point of view:_____

   _____

3. Damian's parents let his brother, who is a year older, do more than Damian gets to do.

   Damian's point of view:_____

   _____

   His parents' point of view: _____

   _____

4. Nick and his scout partner disagree about who should get to sleep in the biggest tent.

   Nick's point of view:_____

   _____

   His partner's point of view:_____

   _____

From Their Point of View

WORKSHEET–PAGE 2

5. Amber has a science test tomorrow. She wants to go skating tonight, but her parents think she should stay home and study.

   Amber's point of view: _____

   _____

   Her parents' point of view: _____

   _____

6. Gabriel's dad doesn't want him to ride his bike along a busy street to the hockey rink. Gabriel doesn't see why he can't do it.

   Gabriel's point of view: _____

   _____

   His dad's point of view: _____

   _____

It's a Choice

Developmental Perspective

As they reach the end of middle childhood, children have increasing opportunities to make choices. Understanding how to identify and assess the importance of choices is a cognitive skill that will prepare them to handle more complex problems.

Objectives

▷ To learn to identify choices

▷ To learn to assess the degree of importance of choices

Materials

▷ A large blank sheet of paper and a pencil for each child

▷ A bottle of glue, a pair of scissors, and several old magazines for each pair of children

▷ Paper and crayons for each child (for the Follow-up Activity)

Procedure

1. Introduce this lesson by asking students to define the word *choice*. Indicate that you will be asking them to think about some aspects of choices. If they strongly agree with what you state, they should raise a hand high. If they somewhat agree with what you state, they should put the hand straight out, and if they disagree with what you state, they should put the hand down.

    ► Everyone has choices.

    ► We make many choices every day.

    ► Some choices are better than others.

    ► The older you get, the more choices you have.

    ► Making choices can be difficult.

    ► Some choices are more important than others.

2. Next have each student find a partner. Distribute a large sheet of paper and a pencil to each child. Give a bottle of glue, a pair of scissors, and several old magazines to each partnership.

3. Ask partners to leaf through their magazines and cut out four pictures that hold some appeal for or interest them. Ask each child to glue two of these pictures on his or her sheet of paper. Then, as partners, have them discuss what choices are associated with each picture and record at least three choices per picture. (For example, they might cut out a picture of someone drinking milk. Examples of choices might include whether or not to drink milk, how often to drink it, what brand of milk to drink, and whether it should be skim, two percent, or whole milk.

4. After they have finished writing the choices, have one partnership join another to discuss their pictures and the choices represented.

5. After sharing the choices, ask children to remain in their groups of four and look at all their choices. Now they should attempt to rank order the choices represented in the pictures from *most important* to *least important*. To do this, they will have to discuss such factors as how the choice would affect them presently and in the future, the relative value of the particular choice to them, and whether the choice would have a major or minor impact on their lives in general. Allow 10–15 minutes for the ranking.

6. To process the activity, discuss the Content and Personalization Questions.

Discussion

Content Questions

1. Was it difficult to think of choices associated with each picture? Were some pictures more difficult than others? If so, what do you think made them more difficult?

2. Do you typically think about all the choices associated with something? If not, do you see any advantage in doing this? (Invite sharing.)

3. What did you experience as you tried to rank order the choices? What factors did you consider as you did the ranking? (Allow time for children to share examples of how they ranked their choices and how they made these decisions.)

Personalization Questions

1. When you make a choice, do you carefully think about all of the factors involved, or do you make your choice quickly without considering all aspects? Which method do you think is best?

2. In your opinion, are there some things you can make choices about rather quickly and others that require more careful deliberation? (Invite sharing of examples.)

3. The next time you have a choice to make, do you think you will do anything differently based on what you learned in this lesson? If so, what?

Follow-up Activity

Have children write the letters CHOICE down the left side of the paper. Beside each letter have them draw a picture or write a word associated with making a choice and starting with that letter.

Does That Make Sense?

Developmental Perspective

Despite their ability to use more complex thinking skills, children in middle childhood still may interpret situations quite literally, thus contributing to the tendency to think irrationally. Irrational thinking negatively affects children in all aspects of their development. Helping them learn to think rationally contributes significantly to their cognitive development.

Objectives

▷ To distinguish between rational and irrational beliefs

▷ To learn how to apply rational beliefs to personal situations

Materials

▷ A Does That Make Sense? Danger Signs Poster (Handout 14)

▷ An envelope of Does That Make Sense? Game Cards (Handout 15) for each group of four children

Procedure

1. Introduce the lesson by displaying the Does That Make Sense? Danger Signs Poster (Handout 14). Use the following examples as a way of illustrating each sign:

   ► Someone refuses to sit by you at lunch. You think: "No one ever wants to eat lunch with me." (Overgeneralizing)

   ► Your older brother won't let you borrow his new CD. You think to yourself: "He is such a mean brother. He should be nicer to me." (Should-ing)

   ► The teacher seems to be watching you while you are taking a test. You think: "She thinks I am cheating on this test." (Mind reading)

   ► Someone steals some of your lunch money from your desk. You think: "Who could do such a thing to me? Someone must really hate me a lot to be so mean." (Personalizing)

   ► Your parents tell you your family is moving to another town. You think: "If I have to move to a different town, I won't be able to stand it. It will just be too hard to leave all my friends. I will be so unhappy all the time I won't be able to do anything." (Exaggerating/low frustration tolerance)

2. Define and discuss the terms *rational* and *irrational*. Explain that *rational* beliefs usually make sense and "fit" with reality. They don't result in upsetting emotions. On the other hand, *irrational* beliefs involve overgeneralizing (thinking that something is always one way or the other), should-ing (making demands about the situation or how others should behave), and mind reading (making assumptions about the situation). Irrational beliefs also involve personalizing (thinking you are the cause of things or that everything is your fault), exaggerating (blowing things out of proportion), and low frustration tolerance (thinking you can't stand something because it is too hard or too uncomfortable). Ask children to identify what makes each of the examples above irrational and ask them to think of more rational responses, such as "Just because someone doesn't sit by me today, it doesn't mean no one ever will."

3. Have children form groups of four and give each group a set of the Does That Make Sense? Game Cards (Handout 15). Explain the following rules for playing the game:

> The dealer shuffles the cards and deals eight cards to each of the four players. Players take turns drawing a card from the player on their right. The object of the game is to match "irrational" cards with their rational counterparts. When a player thinks he or she has a match, that player lays down the pair and explains why the irrational card is irrational and what makes sense about the rational card. That player must also describe a real-life situation in which the rational belief could be used. (For example, if the rational card reads "I can't do everything perfectly," the response could be that the player could remember this the next time before getting upset about making a mistake.) The game continues until two of the four players have completed all their matches (in other words, laid down all their cards).

4. Allow time for groups to play the game, then discuss the Content and Personalization Questions.

Discussion

CONTENT QUESTIONS

1. What is the difference between rational and irrational thinking?
2. Which kind of thinking is better: rational or irrational? Support your response.
3. Do you think there are negative consequences of thinking irrationally? (Invite sharing of examples.)
4. Do you think there are negative consequences of thinking rationally?
5. What kinds of feelings are associated with irrational thinking? With rational thinking?

PERSONALIZATION QUESTIONS

1. Do you think more rationally or irrationally?

2. Have you experienced any negative consequences from thinking irrationally? (Invite sharing.)

3. How can you stop thinking irrationally?

Follow-up Activity

Have children write an "irrational story" about a child who always thinks irrational thoughts and how this affects his or her life. Have them write two endings to the story: one irrational and one rational.

Does That Make Sense?

DANGER SIGNS POSTER

Does That Make Sense?

GAME CARDS—PAGE 1

Leader note: Cut cards apart and put each set in an envelope; give each group of four children one set.

This always happens to me.	Just because this happens sometimes doesn't mean it always happens.
Everything is always unfair.	Sometimes some things are unfair; that's just life.
Nobody likes me.	Just because some people don't like me, that doesn't mean nobody does.
This is the worst thing that could ever happen.	Even though this is a bad thing, it's not the worst thing that could ever happen to me.
I never get to do anything I want to do.	Somethimes I don't get to do things I want to do.
Everyone teases me all the time.	Some kids tease me some of the time.
I'm always a loser.	Sometimes I don't do things well, but that doesn't mean I'm a loser.
I'll die if I can't go to the party.	I wish I could go to the party, but I won't die if I can't go.
She looked at me again. I know she hates me.	Just because she looked at me doesn't mean she hates me.

Does That Make Sense?

GAME CARDS—PAGE 2

My friends should always play what I want to play.	It would be nice if my friends would always let me play what I want, but there's no law that says they have to.
My parents never let me do anything fun.	Once in a while my parents let me do fun things.
I can't stand it if I have to work in that group with those creeps.	I don't like the kids in that group, but I can stand working with them.
I can't stand these school lunches. I'll die if I have to eat another one.	I don't like school lunches, but I won't die if I eat them.
Math is too hard. I can't stand doing these problems.	Math is hard for me, so I just have to work harder to get the problems done.
My parents should always let me do what I want to do.	I wish my parents would always let me do what I want, but probably nobody's parents are like that.
If I don't get picked for that team, I will never forgive the team captain.	I'll be disappointed if I don't get picked for that team, but I guess I'll have to live with it.

Chain Reaction

Developmental Perspective

Although by this time children have more well-developed cognitive abilities, they are also at an age where they will be making increasingly difficult decisions. Because they still tend to think in the present and not project ahead much to the future, they need practice in learning to look at the consequences of their decisions.

Objectives

▷ To learn that decisions have consequences

▷ To identify positive and negative consequences of decisions

Materials

▷ Three paper chains (at least six links per chain)

▷ Three large sheets of paper, three pairs of scissors, three pencils, and glue for each group of three children

Procedure

1. Hold up a paper chain and point out how the pieces are linked together. Discuss the concept of a chain reaction, in which one thing triggers another thing to happen. Indicate that this is how it is with decisions and consequences. To illustrate the relationship, use the following examples, holding a chain in your hand and dropping down one link as you read each decision and consequence.

   ► Situation 1: You didn't do your homework, so on the way to school you asked a friend if you could copy hers. She let you do it. A few days later the teacher gave a pop quiz. Since you hadn't read the material because you copied your friend's homework, you didn't have a clue how to answer the questions on the quiz. As a result, you flunked the quiz. Because you flunked the quiz, your parents made you study every night after school for an hour.

   ► Situation 2: You remember how lonely you were when you first came to this school, so when a new kid joined the class, you invited him to sit at your lunch table and play with you at recess. Later in the week you invited him to join you and a couple other friends for a hike in the woods. You all had a really good time. You continued to include him at school and encouraged him to join your scout troop. After he had been in town several weeks, he asked you to go with his mother and stepfather to a huge amusement park several hours away. You stayed in a motel with a swimming pool and also went to some neat museums. You couldn't believe he asked you to go on such a neat trip, but he said he invited you because you had been so nice to him.

► Situation 3: You decided to let your friends play your older brother's stereo while no one was home. One friend thought he knew a lot about stereos and said the wires to the speakers were not hooked up right. While you went to answer the phone, he switched the wires. Later, when you turned up the volume, the speakers blew out. You decided not to say anything to your brother and hoped he didn't find out that you and your friends had been in his room. However, as soon as your brother turned on his stereo, he immediately accused you and told you that you had to pay for new speakers. Your parents agreed, even though you told them your friend did it. Your parents made you work every Saturday until you had enough money to replace the speakers.

2. Discuss these examples, stressing the fact that decisions can result in both positive and negative consequences, as illustrated. Ask children to share personal examples of both positive and negative consequences of a decision they made recently.

3. Divide children into groups of three. Give each group three large pieces of paper, three pairs of scissors, three pencils, and glue. Instruct groups to cut at least a dozen strips of paper to form a paper chain. After they have cut their strips, have them think of at least three decisions they have made (one per child) and write these on separate strips of paper, putting an asterisk (*) at one corner of the strip. Each child then takes his or her decisions and identifies all the consequences, both positive and negative, and writes these on additional separate strips. Encourage children to discuss the decisions with others in their group, who may be able to identify additional consequences that might have occurred.

4. After this is done, groups start with the first decision and the consequences (in order) and link the strips together to form a paper chain. They do the same for the other decisions and consequences so they end up with one long decision chain (the asterisk designates each new decision).

5. Allow time for groups to share examples of their decisions and consequences, then discuss the Content and Personalization Questions.

Discussion

CONTENT QUESTIONS

1. How are decisions and consequences related?

2. Is it possible to predict consequences? If so, how do you do this?

3. When you think about consequences, do you usually think of the negative ones or the positive ones? Do you think it is important to consider both?

4. Do you think most kids your age consider the consequences of their decisions? If not, do you think this is good or bad?

PERSONALIZATION QUESTIONS

1. Do you typically think about consequences before you make a decision? If so, how do you think this affects your decisions? If not, how do you think this affects your decisions?

2. What did you learn from this lesson that might affect your future decision making?

Follow-up Activity

Have children ask their parents or older siblings the following questions:

► Do you think it is important to consider the consequences before you make a decision? If so, why? If not, why not?

► Can you think of a decision you made in which you did not anticipate the consequences? What happened?

► Do you think your life is better if you think about consequences? Give an example.

Suggest that they write up their interviews and share their results with the rest of the group. An optional activity would be to have children look for examples of consequences/chain reactions in television shows and discuss examples with the group.

Dubious Decisions

Developmental Perspective

At the end of middle childhood, children start to be confronted with decisions that involve moral judgment and that have more serious consequences. Peer pressure, beginning to be stronger at this age, can affect the decisions children make. Learning more about some of the issues children may be confronting can facilitate better decision making.

Objective

▷ To learn more about difficult issues that may affect future decisions

Materials

▷ Chalkboard

▷ Paper and pencils for each group of five children

▷ Resource materials on alcohol, drugs, cigarettes, and theft

Leader note: Resource materials are available from newspapers, magazines, and local substance abuse agencies.

Procedure

1. Divide children into groups of five. Ask each group to brainstorm and list the top five issues they think they will need to make decisions about as they enter middle school. Allow several minutes for discussion, then have groups share. List ideas on the chalkboard.

2. As a large group, try to arrive at some consensus about those issues that could have the most negative consequences, both long term and short term. Assign one of these issues to each group and have groups brainstorm the possible negative outcomes that could result from making poor choices in each of these areas.

3. Next assign each group one of the following issues to research in more detail: alcohol, drugs, cigarettes, and theft. Explain that each group will be asked to give a 15-minute presentation on their topic, following these guidelines:

   ▶ All members of the group must take an active role in the lesson.

   ▶ Information presented must include facts that go beyond common knowledge.

   ▶ Each lesson must use at least one graphic of some sort (chart, graph, display, or poster).

   ▶ Each presentation must include a short creative activity related to the topic to summarize and reinforce the information presented (for example, trivia quiz game, crossword puzzle, make-a-bumper-sticker contest).

4. Give groups several days to prepare their presentations before presenting them to the entire group. After the presentations, process by discussing the Content and Personalization Questions.

Discussion

CONTENT QUESTIONS

1. What did you learn from the presentations? (Encourage sharing of specific facts relative to each topic.)
2. Did you learn about any negative consequences associated with any of these issues?
3. Why do you think kids choose to do things that could be potentially harmful to them?

PERSONALIZATION QUESTIONS

1. Do you think knowing more about these issues will affect your ability to make good decisions about them in the future?
2. Do you know anyone who has made bad decisions about any of these issues? If so, what were the consequences?
3. What do you think you need to remember in order to make good decisions about these or other difficult decisions?

Follow-up Activity

Invite older children into the class to speak about difficult choices they have had to make and to offer advice based on their experiences.

ABOUT THE AUTHOR

Ann Vernon, Ph.D., is Professor and Coordinator of Counseling in the Department of Educational Leadership, Counseling, and Postsecondary Education at the University of Northern Iowa in Cedar Falls. In addition to her university teaching, Dr. Vernon has a private counseling practice, specializing in work with children, adolescents, and their parents. She is the author of numerous articles and several books, including *Counseling Children and Adolescents; Developmental Assessment and Intervention with Children and Adolescents; Thinking, Feeling, Behaving: An Emotional Education Curriculum for Children and Adolescents;* and *What Growing Up Is All About: A Parent's Guide to Child and Adolescent Development* (coauthored with Radhi Al-Mabuk). Dr. Vernon is also Director of the Midwest Center for Rational-Emotive Behavior Therapy and conducts workshops throughout the United States and Canada on applications of REBT with children and adolescents, as well as on other topics relating to work with young people.